PORTRAIT OF
THE BLACK COUNTRY

Portrait of
THE BLACK COUNTRY

by

Harold Parsons

ROBERT HALE · LONDON

© *Harold Parsons 1986*
First published in Great Britain 1986

Robert Hale Limited
Clerkenwell House
Clerkenwell Green
London EC1R 0HT

British Library Cataloguing in Publication Data

Parsons, Harold
    Portrait of the Black Country.—(Portrait series)
    1. Black Country (England)—History
    I. Title
    942.4'9   DA70.B55

ISBN 0-7090-2574-2

Photoset in North Wales by
Derek Doyle & Associates, Mold, Clwyd.
Printed in Great Britain by
St Edmundsbury Press, Bury St Edmunds, Suffolk.
Bound by Hunter & Foulis Limited.

Contents

For my wife Joan,
and Jeff.

Illustrations

Between pages 144 and 145

Railway viaduct at Stourbridge
Tower of the King Edward VI College, Stourbridge
Stuart Crystal, Wordsley
Holy Trinity Church, Wordsley
St Mark's Church, Pensnett
Pit head gear and engine house at the Pensnett Trading Estate
The Vine at Delph, Brierley Hill
The Glynne Arms, Himley
Coronation Gardens, Tipton
Portway Farmhouse, Rowley Regis
Windmill at Ruiton, Gornal

PICTURE CREDITS

All the pictures in this book belong to the author except 1, and 18 which are reproduced by kind permission of Dudley Libraries, and 12, which is reproduced by courtesy of the *Illustrated London News*.

Preface

This book is about the Black Country that its inhabitants know and recognize and includes small localities whose names they strive to perpetuate despite the efforts of government-inspired boundary changes and GPO postal addresses which often place people elsewhere than where they actually live.

Officially the Black Country falls within an area organized in 1966 into the county boroughs of Wolverhampton, Walsall, Dudley, West Bromwich and the new county borough of Warley together with the existing boroughs of Halesowen and Stourbridge. Warley is really a small area on the fringe of Birmingham and at the time virtually unknown to the population of places such as Old Hill and Cradley Heath on which it was foisted. In short, an alien importation!

Then in 1974 an even more monstrous upheaval occurred with further reorganization into the four metropolitan boroughs of Wolverhampton, Walsall, Dudley and Sandwell, all within the West Midlands Metropolitan County, creating a great outcry because Stourbridge and Halesowen certainly did not want to become part of an enlarged Dudley whilst Tipton had no wish to become part of this absurd new Sandwell.

Sandwell really is a nonsense name to bestow on a large part of the Black Country, for as will be shown it derives from nothing more than Sanwell, a mediaeval well. Only for children passing through the education system since 1974 can it have any true meaning and it will take several generations to gain general acceptance in the minds and hearts of the population. As it is one reads in the Press of High Street, Sandwell, when what is meant is High Street, West Bromwich. Must one seriously contemplate West Bromwich Albion Football Club becoming Sandwell Albion?

Postal addresses are a further incongruity. For example, a world-famous Darlaston company is saddled with the address 'Darlaston, Wednesbury', two adjacent but distinctive towns. As far as the West Midlands Metropolitan County is concerned, its fate is immaterial to Black Country folk who belong historically to either South Staffordshire or North Worcestershire.

Readers will appreciate that the foregoing boundary re-organizations of 1966 and 1974 are ignored for the purpose of clarity in order to present a picture of a tightly packed region of over forty definable locations dear to the hearts of their inhabitants and expatriates all over the globe.

A further point should be made. Just as some volumes in this series have a strong emphasis on churches and stately homes, this work is heavily biased in favour of industry. This is as it should be, because that is basically what the Black Country is all about. Where the names of specific firms are mentioned, they either are still in existence or were sufficiently famed in their day to have relevance.

Acknowledgements

I am indebted for information to virtually everyone who has ever written about the Black Country, for research into the region of my birth has been intensified since I became editor of *The Blackcountryman* magazine in 1968.

I especially wish to thank Ron Davies and J. Morris Jones for their help, and also my wife for her constant encouragement especially during expeditions into less familiar territory.

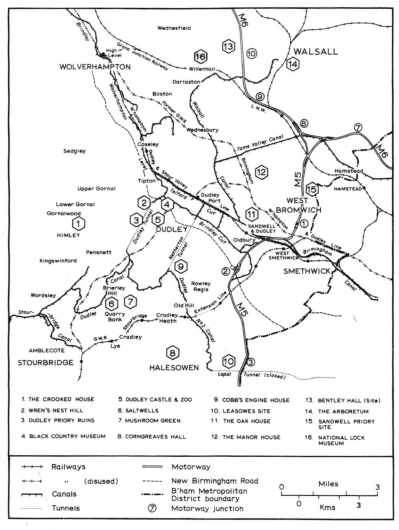

1. THE CROOKED HOUSE	5. DUDLEY CASTLE & ZOO	9. COBB'S ENGINE HOUSE	13. BENTLEY HALL (Site)
2. WREN'S NEST HILL	6. SALTWELLS	10. LEASOWES SITE	14. THE ARBORETUM
3. DUDLEY PRIORY RUINS	7. MUSHROOM GREEN	11. THE OAK HOUSE	15. SANDWELL PRIORY SITE
4. BLACK COUNTRY MUSEUM	8. CORNGREAVES HALL	12. THE MANOR HOUSE	16. NATIONAL LOCK MUSEUM

+—+—+ Railways	════ Motorway
+·+·+ " (disused)	----- New Birmingham Road
┬┬┬ Canals	·—·—· B'ham Metropolitan District boundary
············ Tunnels	⑦ Motorway junction

Miles 0 ——— 3

Kms 0 ——— 3

Based with permission on the Ordnance Survey. Crown Copyright.

1

Definition

The first objective facing anyone writing about the Black Country is to define precisely where it lies, and that is not as easy as might be supposed, even to a native. To Britain at large the region is somewhere in the English Midlands, and it is not unusual for London-based newspapers and Sunday supplements erroneously to include the Potteries which lie well to the north, and the city of Birmingham to the south east. In fact, despite being close neighbours, 'Brummies' tend to be regarded as friendly foreigners. Fraternization is not uncommon!

The main problem in attempting to define the Black Country is that it has no recognized boundaries. It cannot be found on any map, and there are no 'You are now entering the Black Country' signs to be seen, although literally millions of people will have traversed a part of it on the elevated sections of the M5-M6 Midland Links Motorway between junctions 1 and 3 of the M5 and 7 and 10 of the M6 without even being aware that they have done so.

Until the early 1970s many of its inhabitants who had hauled themselves into a degree of affluence preferred to disown it, so that in essence the Black Country started for them in the next locality to that in which they lived. Happily, that way of thinking, born out of a downbeat impression that a Black Country person is 'common', the men being 'strong in the arm but weak in the head', has changed largely through the efforts of organizations such as the Black Country Society and by the rapidly developing Black Country Museum.

Evidence of this change in attitude can be seen in the streets and in advertising copy, for nowadays trades and professions are either prefixing their title 'Black Country Antiques', 'Electrics' or whatever, or stressing their allegiance to the region in print, as do certain breweries and building societies. Moreover, as will be explained, serious attempts are being made to turn the region into a tourist centre, an idea that prior to the 1980s would have been scoffed at. 'They'm saft' would have been the local verdict! Certainly such trends are confounding people who maintain that the Black Country is dying out other than to a small number of fanatics determined to preserve it. Nothing could be further from the truth.

So well and good. But how does one pinpoint the region whilst admitting to its flexibility, a blurring at the edges that has defeated all commentators on the Black Country since it first gained the appellation in the nineteenth century? There is no doubt that any claim will be arguable. What cannot be disputed, however, is that Dudley is the uncrowned capital (unless one can describe a ruined Norman castle on a hill as a crown) standing on a range of hills between five and eight hundred feet above sea level, forming a watershed between the gentle slopes of the eastern part of the region and the steeper western areas. In topographical terms this lofty sweep of ground divides the region in two, so that on whichever side one lives the other is 'over the bank' – or 'bonk' as they say! That is except for the northern end beyond Sedgley, where Wolverhampton merges with Bilston and adjacent towns on more or less level terms.

As to the Black Country as a whole, let us place Wolverhampton at twelve o'clock and work round the perimeter in a clockwise direction. This is not to say that the whole of Wolverhampton is within the region, only its eastern and southern aspects. So round we go: Wednesfield, now part of Wolverhampton, Willenhall and Walsall, down to West Bromwich at three o'clock, Smethwick, Oldbury, then Halesowen, thence to Stourbridge at six o'clock, moving round to Brierley Hill, Sedgley and Kingswinford at around nine o'clock, then back via Himley to Wolverhampton. The outer suburbs of Stourbridge and Halesowen must be excluded.

Given that the Black Country is today an amalgam of linked

townships and villages, each of which struggles to retain a measure of individuality born of a history of isolation so strong that to belong to an adjacent locality is to be labelled as being 'one from off', why does the Black Country exist as a separate if uncharted entity of the West Midlands? The answer lies in part in its geographical position, for there is no major river passing through the area, a vital factor in keeping it relatively free of outside influence in the distant past when waterways were the favoured means of travel, exploration and eventual trade and intermingling.

Add to this the fact that the area was once dense forest and chase, with its forbidding dorsal ridge, and one can appreciate why the scanty population of ancient times saw little merit in penetration when it was easy to bypass. The Romans certainly gave it a miss, at least in strength: their Watling Street, built in A.D. 50, runs well to the east and some eight miles north of Wolverhampton, swinging west towards Viroconium near Shrewsbury, whilst at the southern extremity their main route appears to have been the so-called Ryknild Street, which passes through the heart of modern Birmingham. Here were two prongs by which to link with their comrades in the Severn Valley and the much-prized saltpans at Droitwich without troubling to cross the future Black Country.

As for the Danes, they too seem to have made little impact, the Danelaw being at its closest in the East Midlands. However, this may not have been for want of trying, for a decisive battle is said to have taken place at Wednesfield in A.D. 910 when the Anglo-Saxons were victorious. Admittedly Wednesfield (or Wodensfield after the pagan god Woden) was not the only place hereabouts where battle was joined, for neighbouring Willenhall has a similar claim, but Wednesfield it is which cherished the story to the extent of portraying the battle on the civic seal of the former urban district council. One should beware though in imagining a battle in a modern context since in reality it probably involved very few people. Whatever the size or strength of the encounter, or indeed if it happened at all, there is no evidence of Danish occupation of the area we know as the Black Country, although, like the Romans, they were close to its elastic boundaries.

What of the Anglo-Saxons? Well, it is that combination of Germanic races which forms the peg on which twentieth-century

Black Country folk hang their heritage. As part of the kingdom of Mercia which had emerged by the eighth century, they had taken over from the Celtic-speaking peoples who had been the first to occupy the area albeit in sparse numbers. (Here one ignores prehistoric times, for as recently as January 1985 more than a hundred flint flakes and knives were excavated near West Bromwich and dated as being from 6000 B.C., the large quantity suggesting a settlement.) The evidence for Anglo-Saxon influence on the shaping of what was to be known as the Black Country is two-fold: the high incidence of place-names of Saxon origin and its dialect.

When the Saxons cut clearings in the forest, they called them 'leahs' or 'leys', and since it was their practice to name a settlement after its founder, it follows that Dudley was the ley of a man called Dudda, Sedgley after someone called Sedda, Cradley after Cradda and so on.

Then we have the evidence of the Black Country dialect, which local historians stoutly maintain is basically Anglo-Saxon and not the refined 'King's English' of the early universities. The dialect is hard for strangers to understand. Indeed, national radio and television won't tolerate it unless it is watered down considerably as several playwrights have discovered – although they will permit Liverpool 'Scouse', Newcastle 'Geordie' and even broad Scots. Come to that, even the local media will suffer it only in small doses. Be that as it may, the dialect is more genuinely Old English than can be found elsewhere in England, and since Chaucer wrote his *Canterbury Tales* in the fourteenth century using a version of the Mercian dialect, Black Country readers can identify with parts of his writing because they speak or 'spaken' it. The suffix 'en' is one example, for older Black Country people especially will talk of 'gooin' [going] up the housen'. 'Dun yo' know*en* who's got old Ayli's place?' they might enquire, whilst 'Just watch the folk*en* all go by' appears in an ancient rhyme. 'Aferd' for 'afraid' and 'keche' for 'catch' are other Chaucerian examples.

This is not the place to give a glossary of the hundreds of dialect words used by natives of the region; suffice to say that it is still spoken. Whereas twenty years ago a child would get 'a clout round the ear'ole' for speaking it, nowadays it is considered respectable and even actively encouraged in schools as part of heritage studies. Local dialect comedians and poets are encouraged and find ready audiences, and several paperback books of dialect work have been published. Even parts of the Old Testament have been transcribed and welcomed in print by layman and clergy alike. Since most readers will be familiar with the beginning of Genesis, try this round the tongue to get the flavour: 'Ter start everythin' off, God med the wairld. Mind yo', 'e couldn't see ennythin' 'cuz it wuz all dark, soo 'e sed, "Let's a' sum lite", an' the lite cum, an' 'e wor 'arf plaised wi' it ...' No wonder the printer said it was like setting a foreign language!

Volumes of Black Country jokes find favour, although here one finds that a certain Irishness has crept in. This is because during the eighteenth and nineteenth centuries Irishmen came to dig the canals and later construct railway embankments as well as bring their brawn to the heavy industries. No commentary on the Black Country would be complete without examples from the hundreds of dialect jokes frequently based, oddly enough, on death and funerals but not indicative of undue morbidity.

A man attending the funeral of his wife was asked by the undertaker to ride in the same car as his mother-in-law. 'I'll do it to oblige,' he said. 'But don't forget, you're going to spoil my day.'

Following the cremation of her husband, a widow had the ashes placed in an egg-timer. As she explained: 'He didn't do any work when he was alive, and I'm going to see as he makes himself useful now he's jed [dead].'

In this context my wife often relates a bizarre telephone conversation she had when we lived at Dudley. Without any preamble a male voice said, 'When are you coming to fetch her?' She said, 'I think you have the wrong number,' but he ignored her and went on 'When are you coming to fetch her? It's me wife, Alice. her's been here now three days, you know.' 'I'm sorry,' my wife repeated. 'You've got the wrong number,' whereupon he said, 'It's the mortuary, ay it?' A true story of the 1960s with the dialect refined for the sake of clarity.

As for that Irish element, there is the Black Country man who complained of the council: 'They collect the rates but they don't do nothing. There's holes in our road two foot high.'

Then there's the woman who came to her front door and

complained: 'There! The milkman's been and gone and not come again'. One knows what she means.

If it seems that overlong emphasis has been given to the dialect, it is because of its importance within the life of the community, although it varies slightly from locality to locality. In the Halesowen district, for example, it is spoken in a sort of sing-song cadence with an uplift at the end of sentences. Whatever its detractors might say, the dialect is in regular use. One has only to go into back-street public houses and listen to the locals gossiping over darts or dominoes, or overhear British-born sons and daughters of West Indian and Asian immigrants chattering away in broad Black Country, to be not only convinced but bemused.

Since this is not intended as a concise history, it is necessary that, having dealt with the all-important Anglo-Saxon heritage, we should jump forward to consider the Black Country as such. The Industrial Revolution of the eighteenth century which began at Coalbrookdale, Shropshire, led eventually to a spillover into the area that came to be known as the South Staffordshire Coalfield. The first major move came from North Wales when John ('Iron Mad') Wilkinson came from Wrexham to set up a coal-smelting furnace at Bradley, near Bilston, in 1757. He came, as later did a host of ironmasters and entrepreneurs, because of an abundance of coal, iron ore and limestone – principally coal which outcropped at Bilston and adjoining towns as well as in parts of Dudley, and at Brierley Hill on the western side of the ridge. Outcrop coal had been known of for centuries, and records show it to have been mined in the region during the thirteenth century.

However, the impact of coke-smelting was dramatic, and a local historian was to write of 'mine after mine and ironworks after ironworks springing up – and a great influx of workmen from the earlier opened mines of Shropshire and Wales'.

The deep coal as yet unexploited proved to be of massive proportions in South Staffordshire and gave rise to the term 'Ten Yard Coal', seams being up to thirty feet thick. This is not to suppose that it lay in one solid mass, for it consisted of a number of layers of different characteristics and qualities of which only experienced miners can tell the difference. Here lay the real riches of the emerging Black Country.

Ask how the Black Country got its name and more than likely
the answer will be by reason of its great profusion of chimneys
belching out smoke from ironworks and furnaces, combined with
a general incidence of grime and dirt which typified the region by
the end of the eighteenth century. But that is only part of the
reason, for other parts of the country also had high
concentrations of industry at the time when the region was so
christened. The other, perhaps major part of the answer is in the
South Staffordshire Coalfield itself, shaded grey or black on
geographical maps of the time. To be precise, this area is the true
Black Country, yet even taking this criterion, faults in the coal
measures produced inconsistencies so that as late as 1895 it was
being suggested that worthwhile coal seams existed outside the
originally designated coalfield to the west and at a greater depth.

This proved to be the case, the result being the sinking of the
last colliery in the Black Country to exploit the thick coal:
Baggeridge Colliery, close to Himley, for long the seat of the earls
of Dudley, struck coal twenty-four feet thick, and it was to be
mined until the seams petered out and led to closure in 1968.
This was the end of deep mining in the region, a saddening event
which led to the striking of a commemorative medallion to mark
the demise of the last working pit in the Black Country. *That's*
how strongly local folk felt about it.

Subsequently considerable open-cast mining activity has
taken place with varying success, and in 1984 attempts were
made to mine an established nature reserve in this way. The
outcry was such that the project was dropped, which is not to say
that it won't be renewed, for the lure of mineral wealth may well
triumph over those who seek to protect wild life and flora.
Moreover, there is no doubt that there is still plenty of deep coal
beneath the Black Country. Whether it will ever be worth getting
is another matter.

We have seen then that the region got its name by reason of its
ironworks, furnaces and mineral wealth, but *when* did it acquire
the name Black Country? William Cobbett, the radical
politician and writer who lectured in the region in 1830, called it
the Iron Country, a reasonable enough description. But, so far as
one can tell, it was first given the title Black Country in print in a
book entitled *All Round the Wrekin* by Walter White, in 1860, an
unlikely source since the Wrekin in Shropshire is over twenty

miles distant. A certain William Hawkes Smith almost claimed the honour in a clumsily entitled work of 1838 with his reference to a 'black compartment ... sable tinted province', whilst a railway guide of 1838 referred to 'the Staffordshire Mining District'.

However, the name actually appeared in 1868 as the title of a book, *The Black Country and its Green Borderland* (reprinted 1976), written by a man named Elihu Burritt, who at the time was the American Consul in Birmingham. It is significant that he too by virtue of his chosen title edged his bets in defining the region by adding 'green borderland'. His opening words, 'The Black Country, black by day and red by night', have passed into local lore and reflected what others thought and wrote, for many eminent men were to make it their business to visit the region in its first industrial heyday and set down their often lurid descriptions. It was Hell on Earth, it was the place where the Devil died in despair in seeing an establishment to rival his own. A locally famous piece of doggerel runs:

> When Satan stood on Brierley Hill
> And far around him gazed,
> He said, 'I never shall again
> At Hell's flames be amazed.'

Thomas Carlyle wrote in 1824; 'A frightful scene ... a dense cloud of pestilential smoke hangs over it forever ... and at night the whole region burns like a volcano spitting fire from a thousand tubes of brick. But oh the wretched thousands of mortals who grind out their destiny there!'

James Nasmyth (engineer and inventor of the steam hammer), writing of a visit in 1830: 'The earth seems to have been turned inside out. Its entrails strewn about; nearly the entire surface of the ground covered with cinder heaps and mounds ... By day and night the country is glowing with fire, and the smoke of ironworks hovers over it.'

Lovers of Charles Dickens will recall in *The Old Curiosity Shop* the fearful journey made by Nell and her grandfather through just such a scene, believed in fact to be the Black Country, when 'tall chimneys crowding on each other ... poured out their plague of smoke ... obscured the light, and made foul the melancholy air'.

All of these writers in one way or another portrayed the 'not a blade of grass' imagery, yet anyone who has seen an area of dereliction – and there is always plenty of that in the Black Country – knows how rapidly greenery begins to appear, so a degree of poetic licence must be accorded even though the region was horrible enough not to require exaggeration. Even in those days though, parts of the Black Country were not all that black, as this account of 1844 shows, written by an unknown hand and concerning the western areas around Halesowen: 'Everywhere cottages and mud hovels met the eye in the most picturesque situations. The whole population of this beauteous region being, without distinction of sex, nailers.' But as he nears the coalfield he is compelled to add: 'Lanes, instead of being pleasant and shady, become mere ravines, as if in some convulsion of the earth the solid rock has been rent assunder.'

Thus from writers of the time the Black Country came to life in capital letters, so to speak, and we know what it was like, but it was never one mass of mines, for many districts had – and to some extent have today – diverse specialist skills and crafts, and of these we shall learn in later chapters. Although many locations will be mentioned, it should be remembered that they are all cheek by jowl, distinguishable only by roadsigns. Yet that age-old feeling of individuality has continued to exist in people's minds. For instance, when as a lad I went to work in Wolverhampton, I was immediately nicknamed 'Moon' because I came from Dudley and everybody knew that Dudley had a moon of its own. So has Tipton, but that is earthbound, and on clear nights generations of drunks have tried to fish it out of the canal.

Today's Black Country folk are still apt to be somewhat clannish, liable to be blunt but good hearted. Like as not a woman will call you 'me luvva' regardless of sex or status, and the first reaction to a visitor is to put the kettle on. That is, once they know you to be genuine, for alas it is no longer safe to open the door to strangers.

2

Before the Industrial Revolution

It was necessary to leap quickly into the nineteenth century in order to indicate how and approximately when the Black Country acquired its name. Now it is necessary to backtrack and look at earlier development within the region to see how its natural resources and the talents of its people were utilized, for it must not be supposed that the Industrial Revolution spreading from North Wales and Shropshire brought about a change of scene virtually overnight. Far from it! There was already widespread and diverse activity, and even the term 'Industrial Revolution' should be qualified, for in fact there have been several (that in the cotton industry for example). The Industrial Revolution as applied to the Black Country is basically concerned with the extraction of minerals and the production of iron with coal, using steam as a source of power.

But before coming to that, let us take a quick flip through the centuries from those early Brit/Saxon settlements when the area consisted of forest and heath linking up with Cannock Chase to the east and Kinver forest to the west to provide a vast blanket of vegetation crossed by rough tracks and dotted with tiny clearings so that a Dr Who-type time-traveller would have seen nothing to suggest its future significance. The awaiting riches lay beneath the soil. Fortunately there are two minor rivers scarcely worthy of the name and hardly given a second glance today but before the age of steam utilized out of all proportion to their size, as indeed were their tiny tributaries. One is the River Tame, which meanders over the gentle gradients of the eastern slopes, and the other is the River Stour which flows to the west. Thus, water falling on the eastern side of the Black Country ridge reaches the North Sea via the River Trent and that falling on the western side reaches the Bristol Channel via the River Severn.

Each river had several crude waterwheels at the time of Domesday. The appearance of three monastic priories in the twelfth century added to their number, and the monks brought advances in agriculture and husbandry throughout their extensive lands, doubtless spurring local folk to new endeavours. Sandwell Priory was founded in about 1130 by the Benedictine Order in the forest of West Bromwich close to the Sanwell, from 'sanctus fons', holy well or spring. It was suppressed in 1526, when it was said to be already in a ruinous condition.

Dudley Priory was rather more substantial, founded in about 1180 following a grant of land by the Norman landowner who inhabited the castle. It was of the Cluniac Order of Benedictine monks and became affiliated to Wenlock Abbey in Shropshire. It was very much under the thumb, and eye, of the castle, being 'about a bow-shoot westward'. Local lore has it that a tunnel once linked the two, an unlikely supposition. This priory also suffered the fate of dissolution, although not until the superior home fell in 1540. Happily its ruins stand today in Priory Park for anyone to walk among and admire, the subject of a preservation order. In these more history-conscious times it is natural that they should be preserved, but such considerations did not always apply, for in the eighteenth century, if not earlier, the ruins suffered the indignity of being used, with crude additional workshops, for various trades including tanning and thread-manufacture. Even in the nineteenth century it was found to house workmen who ground glass and polished fire-irons.

The third monastery, that at Halesowen, was founded in about 1214 as a convent for the white canons of St Mary's who belonged to a then newish order, the Premonstratensians, named after their place of origin in Picardy. An energetic community of considerable power, they suffered the fate of the others under Henry VIII, and although a farmhouse was built into the ruins, it was at least more in keeping with the pastoral pursuits of the monks than the indignity inflicted at Dudley. Still part of a farm today; it is not accessible to the public and would in fact be considered as being outside the Black Country proper. Even so, for some three hundred years its influence extended well into the region across to Walsall and Wednesbury when, sometime in the thirteenth century, the church at Waleshale with its chapel at Wednesbury was granted to the abbot and convent of Halesowen.

Turning to Wolverhampton, it is possible to go even further back in terms of religious penetration. What happened was that in 994, in the reign of Aethelred II, the Lady Wulfruna (also spelt Wulfrun) used part of a grant of lands to endow the monastery of St Mary at Heantun, whose canons also held lands at Wednesfield and Willenhall now in the Black Country, and elsewhere. After the Conquest Lady Wulfruna's privileges were confirmed by the Conqueror, but the church was to pass through many changes and become St Peter's before the deanery was joined to that of Windsor in 1479, an arrangement that lasted until 1846. The important point to come through to today is that the land was given to Lady Wulfruna by the King in 985, and it is on this fact that 'Wulfrun Heantun', transposed to Wolverhampton, celebrated its millennium in 1985.

Mention has been made of Dudley Castle, a structure that could almost warrant a chapter in itself. Perched on a mound atop a limestone ridge, its fourteenth-century ruined keep is visible for miles on the eastern side, as anyone who has travelled the main Wolverhampton-Birmingham railway line or the stilted motorway network will have noticed, but it is not visible from the west, high ground intervening. The castle is basically of Saxon origin for the Domesday survey tells us that Earl Edwin held it in Edward the Confessor's reign but that in 1086 'William holds Dudley and there is his castle.' This was the famed William Fitz Ansculf, and the Conqueror must have held him in high regard for he gave him twenty-five manors in Staffordshire, fourteen in Worcestershire and five in Warwickshire, all within a dozen miles of the castle, also manors elsewhere in the country. The line of succession and the immense power of the castle in its heyday are too involved to enter into here, though well documented. Suffice to mention a few highlights, or lowlights, according to one's point of view.

By the sixteenth century the 'Castle Dudleys' were among the most influential in the land. The castle came into the possession of John Dudley, who already owned Warwick and was to become Duke of Northumberland. He rebuilt the castle in the 1540s, but he came unstuck when he tried to put Lady Jane Grey on the throne and paid the supreme penalty. Queen Elizabeth visited the castle in 1575, and ten years later, when it was decided to move Mary, Queen of Scots, from Tutbury, a visit was made to the castle to see if it was suitable for her imprisonment. It wasn't! The visiting official gave a condemning report, complaining of a lack of 'table boords, cupboordes, fourmes, stools and bedsteds'. The brewing vessels were 'somewhat decayed' and the 'water must be set owt of the dikes without the gates and yet some will say that the pump which standeth in the middle of the court yf yt be cleaned would furnish sufficient and good water, but I find others that doubt thereof'. How strange that a place of such importance should be so lacking in amenity, yet fit to receive a reigning queen but not an imprisoned one. Was a bad impression given deliberately? We shall never know, but the royal prisoner went to Chartley instead.

During the Civil War the castle was a Royalist garrison until captured by Cromwell's soldiers in 1646, when it was rendered untenable as a garrison, the residential part being largely untouched. It was not abandoned, although the main seat of the Dudley lords was to be at Himley on the western edge of today's Black Country. In fact, it was inhabited until the night of 24 July 1750, when a disastrous fire occurred. A contemporary report said that it burned for three days and folk would not go near on account of the gunpowder thought to be on the premises. The eastern part of the roof, being mainly of lead, ran down the hill and set fire to the hillside.

Luke Booker, Vicar of Dudley and a man ever ready to put pen to paper, wrote in a subsequent history: 'Never perhaps was it [the castle] so magnificent a spectacle as when, illuminated by the consumption of its own glories, it gleamed far and wide, a sublime though melancholy pageant of departing grandeur! Its coronal of battlemented towers was broke [sic], its ceilings of vermilion and floors of cedar served but as fuel to complete the fall.' It is said that the fire was caused by counterfeit coiners working secretly in the dungeons and vaults of the castle, but if it was still a residence, surely someone would have known.

However, not to overrun the tale we must return to the period when, having established their monasteries, the Normans turned their attentions to the building of churches. This they did with considerable fervour, and a number of parish churches in the region still have identifiable features from those times. Then, too, markets were granted. Wolverhampton's market charter of 1258 confirmed the right to hold a market apparently already in existence, but it seems that Dudley possessed a market charter of earlier date, for in 1261 there was a lawsuit complaining that the market in Wolverhampton would unfairly compete with Dudley's, despite being some six miles distant. The case was arguable, and in true British compromise the Dean of Wolverhampton allowed Dudley folk freedom of tolls in his Wolverhampton market. As recently as 1984 a new Wolverhampton market was challenged as being too close to the existing, invoking an early charter. As the dialect might express it, 'Yo' cor dew just what you'd amind.'

The first major development beyond the ordinary affairs of agriculture and livestock was in the woollen industry. Possibly by reason of its central position and relatively close proximity to Shropshire and Wales, Wolverhampton was by the fourteenth century an important wool-collecting centre. Here it was processed and made into coarse cloth. Many local men made fortunes and had warehouses in London, the goods being shipped to the Continent. Significantly, a woolpack features on the town's coat of arms, but the trade undoubtedly spread across the region because there were Woolpack inns bearing the sign of the Drapers' Company in most towns. Moreover, in Salop Street, Dudley, on the main road which follows the line of the limestone ridge to Wolverhampton, there stood until the 1970s a pub with the unusual name 'The Welsh Go-By', and I can visualize the white-painted lettering on the windowpanes. Did the Welsh really drive their sheep as far as Dudley market?

Now to the mineral extraction which was to spawn the Black Country proper. Coal had been mined at shallow depths for generations, and thirteenth-century documents refer to coalpits in Wednesbury, Halesowen, where it was mined by monks, Sedgley and elsewhere, but only for domestic purposes for at that time there seemed no other use for it. Iron ore was also mined in Wednesbury and other places from about the same period, and crude wrought iron was produced by laboriously smelting the ore with charcoal and working it into shape by hand-hammers or, as later, water-powered hammers – which is where the rivers Tame and Stour came into their own. This method consumed considerable quantities of timber, and when the first charcoal blast furnace was introduced into the Black Country – at West Bromwich in the 1590s – timber began to disappear even more rapidly. But there was no stopping the progress of the iron industry, and the seriousness of the timber situation can be gleaned from the fact that Richard Foley's five furnaces, nine forges and slitting mills are said to have consumed 19,320 trees in 1636 alone. Incidentally, Richard Foley is widely credited with having been the first in the region to erect a slitting mill for producing easily workable nail rods. This mill, although on the River Stour, was not in the Black Country but some four miles downstream at Kinver. One way and another, the Foley family were to have considerable impact on the region, and they are commemorated today in schools and by street names.

It is hardly surprising that, as the seventeenth century advanced, timber supplies began to dwindle and the authorities began to sit up and take notice: the navy in particular, being a major user of timber for shipbuilding, made appropriate warning noises, and attempts were made to find an alternative fuel. Enter the figure of Dud Dudley (1599-1684). His book *Metallum Martis* published in 1665 sets out the problem in revealing the extent of ironworking, especially nailmaking in the mid-seventeenth century when he wrote that there were nearly twenty-thousand smiths of all sorts within a ten-mile radius of Dudley. He calculated that it required two loads (or two cords) of wood 'at the least' to make a load of charcoal and that to produce fifteen tons of pig iron for forty weeks required twelve hundred loads of charcoal. The urgency of finding a new fuel was not lost to him, and he was in a position to try to do something about it.

Dud Dudley, a bastard son of the Lord Dudley of the time, had been well educated and placed in charge of three of his father's ironworks on Pensnett Chase. His attempts to smelt iron with coal as a fuel were numerous and protracted and, although he took out patents, positively claimed to have made iron with 'pit coal' and carefully set down his experiments in *Metallum Martis*, no historian has yet become convinced that his endeavours were successful. Certainly nothing came of his work commercially, and the credit for solving fell to another man of Black Country birth. His name was Abraham Darby and, as the world knows, he successfully smelted iron with coke as fuel in 1709: alas not in his native region but at Coalbrookdale, Shropshire. Although Darby saved the iron industry from dependence on charcoal and earned immortality in the process, and although he didn't slap restrictive patents on his discovery as had Dud Dudley, some forty years were to pass before the Black Country made positive use of it. Whilst there are several reasons for this, the key to unlock Black Country coal measures had been turned.

In addition to coal and iron, the region was rich in clay: not any old clay but high-quality fireclay rated among the best in the world and extending in a belt from Stourbridge through Brierley Hill and Pensnett to Kingswinford. This clay plus an abundance of coal was a surefire target for the founding of a glass industry, and it is popularly supposed that Huguenot glassmakers, probably coming to England from Lorraine to escape religious persecution, were the first to see the potential. Not that they arrived direct in a sort of gold-rush stampede, for their movements about the country were considerable before they heard of these ideal mineral deposits. Like the iron trade they faced the restrictions of timber shortage, and the presence of coal for their fires and a type of clay suitable for their pots, lying together for the taking, must have seemed too good to be true. The exact date of their arrival in the area is uncertain but the earliest families to arrive were named Tysack and Henzie, and the Kingswinford parish register of 1612 records the baptism of a young Tysack, whilst three years later babies born to the Henzies were baptized at Oldswinford, Stourbridge. Glassmaking remains an important industry in the modern Black Country, and more detailed reference will be made in a later chapter.

Coal! Iron ore! Fireclay! The mineral wealth of the future Black Country was phenomenal for to the list must be added one more – limestone! You couldn't miss it. Nor can you to this day, the Wren's Nest hill at Dudley being a limestone outcrop that all the quarrying of centuries has failed to level. From the earliest times limestone was used as a building material – Dudley Castle is constructed of it – but it had another use discovered by the early ironmakers. Dud Dudley (Yes, him again!) made in his *Metallum Martis* one of the first documented references to limestone being used as a flux in the smelting of iron ore. Add the use of lime for agricultural purposes and it is not difficult to see how the limestone industry prospered in the region until early in the present century. Quarried and mined, it has left awesome caverns and widespread problems of subsidence with which present-day authorites have to cope. Morever, it was rich in fossils.

Fossils from the Wren's Nest are to be found in most collections throughout the world. The most famous is the Calymene blumenbachi, once so common that it was called the 'Dudley Locust' but now one of the rarer specimens likely to be found. This trilobite appears on the town's coat of arms, and a four-million-year heritage, give or take a few, can't be bad. We shall see later how the old limestone workings and the Wren's Nest hill add to the town's attractions.

An outstanding event in industrial history occurred in 1712, when a steam pumping engine, the most advanced technical achievement in its field and the first in the world to boast a cylinder and piston, was installed at a mine on the Tipton side of Dudley Castle – the precise spot is unauthenticated. It was the brainchild of a Cornish engineer and inventor, Thomas Newcomen (1663-1729), and was erected at Tipton to pump water, highlighting a problem that was to bedevil Black Country mining operations for more than two hundred years. The Newcomen engine proved particularly suited to the Black Country since it consumed a great deal of coal, and of that there was no shortage. The region is proud to have been the home of the engine, and a full-size replica has been installed at the Black Country Museum probably within a mile of the original site.

In tandem with mineral extraction, different localities developed their own crafts and skills in the manufacture of a wide range of goods in excess of the needs of local consumption. Just as wool was exported, so was other merchandise, and the inadequacies of conveyance by packhorse to the Severnside inland ports of Bewdley and Bridgnorth were infuriatingly slow, subject to theft and not least to breakage. One can imagine glassmakers in particular uttering the Black Country equivalent of 'botheration' as yet another consignment was reported shattered! Nevertheless, the River Severn was the region's main trade artery, so near yet so far, and the Stour too small to be of use, although an engineer named Andrew Yarranton claimed in

1665 to have made it navigable from Stourbridge to Kidderminster. To look at the tight curves of the little river today as it snakes through meadowland from Staffordshire into Worcestershire, the claim seems unbelievable.

Such conditions had to be tolerated for many years longer, as is evident from a report of 1726 which describes the Wolverhampton to Birmingham road as ruinous in winter and in places almost impassable – and that was a major thoroughfare! It was no better in 1745, when John Wesley complained of the state of the high road where his horse stuck fast in a 'quagmire' near Wednesbury Town End, and from which he had to be rescued by his friends by the light of candles. At last the Turnpike Acts gave hope of better things, the earliest to affect the Black Country being in 1727, when the road from Birmingham to Wednesbury, with a branch to Walsall, was turnpiked. Turnpike roads were constructed from Birmingham to Stourbridge in 1753 and to Dudley in 1761, yet from the start they brought only patchy improvement, for tolls were usually let in groups to the highest bidder and, as in any such business venture (witness today's motorway service areas), some were good, others poor. Added to which people objected to paying tolls, gates were uprooted, keepers physically attacked, so that by and large transportation of goods remained a hazardous experience. It is hardly surprising that frustrated landowners who possessed the mineral wealth of the Black Country – in particular the Earl of Dudley – should join with industrial entrepreneurs to seek a better means of moving raw materials and finished goods. They looked to the Duke of Bridgewater and his hitherto unknown engineer, James Brindley, who in the 1760s was building near Manchester the wonder of the age – a canal.

By this time, as already stated, John Wilkinson had erected his furnace at Bradley, Bilston. T.S. Ashton's book *The Industrial Revolution* places its beginnings in 1760, although later researchers consider it to have been earlier. As with most events of a flexible nature, there can be no positive date as far as the Black Country is concerned. It would seem reasonable to leave this chapter at the point where Wilkinson arrived in the region. After all, did he not found what was to become known as the 'mother furnace'? The mother of the Black Country's *own* industrial revolution.

3

Through to the Twentieth Century

The first canal to benefit the Black Country was the Birmingham Canal which wove its way through the region to a point north of Wolverhampton (Autherley) where it joined the Staffordshire and Worcestershire Canal, both completed in 1772. The Birmingham Canal was winding for two reasons, neither of which was any consolation to boatmen: to avoid hills as far as possible and to pass as close to as many mines and ironworks as the twists and turns would allow. Despite such shortcomings, later to be ironed out, the canal was a success from the beginning, and almost every work on the subject relates how immediately the first section was opened to Wednesbury in 1769 the price of coal to Birmingham fell from 13 shillings to 7 shillings a ton. Such a reduction over so short a distance underlies the high cost of road haulage.

It was largely Birmingham manufacturers who financed this canal, whilst the Staffs and Worcs – to give it its abbreviated name – was promoted first by a group of businessmen of no great distinction followed by influential landowners who came forward with capital. Among them was Sir Edward Littleton, who chaired the enterprise and in 1835 became Lord Hatherton. 'Hatherton' is a name still much associated with the region. This canal passed to the west of the Black Country, and no doubt to his great chagrin neither came close enough to the dorsal ridge of the Black Country to satisfy Lord Dudley, so in 1776 Acts were passed for two more canals, one from Stourbridge to join the

Staffs and Worcs at Stourton to the west of Stourbridge, the other beginning the climb up to Dudley. These combined to enable a more effective movement of goods and materials, but the ridge itself was too steep for locks and remained a stubborn obstacle to the construction of a short east/west canal route.

The solution was breathtaking for its time and something of a marvel even now considering the interest displayed by visitors. It was the construction of a tunnel nearly two miles long to pass beneath Dudley and link with the canal systems on either side. Instead of taking the estimated three years to construct, it took seven. So many difficulties were encountered that the original contractors went bankrupt, and because two different contractors were involved, it suffers a slight change of direction. Completed in March 1792, it soon proved a bottleneck, mainly because to save cost it was built without a towpath so that boatmen had to lie on their back and propel the boat through by pushing with their feet against the roof, which was less than six feet in height – hence its popular name, 'Legging Tunnel'. When I went through in 1964, during a publicity trip organized by a group of enthusiasts who had formed a preservation society to save the tunnel from closure, pushing by dozens of hands against the slimy walls achieved the same objective as legging in getting the boat through. However, in its heyday the absence of a towing path created enormous problems: horses had to be walked overland to the exit, a one-way system was essential, and with queues of boats waiting at either end there were unacceptable delays and not a little fisticuffs among frustrated boatmen.

The Lord Dudley of the day had an additional motive for burrowing a canal through the ridge, for at the Tipton end it quickly reached his limestone excavations, and in the 1790s an underground branch canal was started from the main tunnel, extending as the working face extended, presenting a perfect answer to getting limestone on the move. So successful was this project that three such waterways were eventually completed – two striking out under Dudley Castle hill and the other reaching 785 yards towards the Wren's Nest mines in about 1815, so linking up the two main extraction areas by waterways. These side canals have long been lost to present-day preservationists but that 1964 attempt to save the main tunnel from being walled up was successful, and it is true to say that but for the efforts of those few dedicated people the Black Country Museum would have been short of one of its chief attractions, for the eastern entrance is virtually on museum property. Unfortunately it has not been possible to navigate the whole length of the tunnel for some years because of the deteriorating brick linings, although the British Waterways Board have affirmed their intention to carry out repairs when funds permit; meanwhile trips have been made as far as the limestone workings, no fewer than eighty thousand visitors making the journey during 1984. Moreover, the amount of interest generated has led to the construction of a new branch tunnel into what is known as the Singer Cavern. Sixty-five yards long, it is the first such tunnel to be built in Britain in over a century and underlines the tremendous interest in this aspect of the Black Country's heritage.

The canal mania of the eighteenth century continued well into the nineteenth, by which time, just as early motorways proved inadequate, the early narrow canals could not cope with the volume of traffic. Something had to be done and one of the major steps taken was to appoint Thomas Telford to survey Brindley's Birmingham-Wolverhampton canal. He advocated the shortening of the waterway by straightening, lowering its summit to reduce the number of locks and building a new reservoir. His suggestions were accepted and by 1838 the master engineer's 'straight' canal had reduced the distance by about seven miles: bearing in mind that the distance between the two towns (Birmingham was not a city then) is only about thirteen miles, it was a big slice to take out, doubtless appreciated by all concerned. Moreover, it had double towpaths, embankments and spectacular cuttings, being described at the time as 'unsurpassed in stupendous magnificence by any similar work in the world'. They certainly knew how to gild the lily in those days without the help of high-powered public relations agencies, but visitors to Smethwick will still find the cutting impressive.

By 1837 the railway era had dawned when the Grand Junction Railway opened between Birmingham and Warrington, crossing the eastern part of the Black Country, so that Telford's cut might appear to have been too late as speculators and manufacturers rushed to extend this new marvel, but its worth has to be set against the tremendous volume of materials and goods on the move, far more than the fledgling railways could hope to handle. One can hardly conceive today the degree of activity confined within this geographically small area of the English Midlands. Even as late as 1850 canal improvements were in hand, the most notable being the opening in 1858 of the 3,027-yard Netherton Tunnel, built, belatedly one might think, to reduce congestion on the Dudley legging tunnel. This new tunnel has towpaths on both sides, making it the widest in the land, and it was illuminated by gas (later by electricity). It has the distinction of being the last canal tunnel to be built during the canal age. It has been repaired and is open today.

From the first canal to the last, all those within the Black Country are narrow; hence commercial boats, now of course all in private hands for leisure use, are 'narrow boats' and to refer to them as barges is to invite derision – just one of those things Black Country enthusiasts feel strongly about! But before leaving the canals I have a personal recollection to add concerning the private arms or 'basins' which factories sited near to a canal had constructed to enable loading/off-loading inside the works. As a boy I worked at a Wolverhampton factory with just such a basin. They employed a man nicknamed Noah (what else?) to ferry laden narrow boats to the railway goods yard wharf, but in addition boats belonging to commercial carrying companies would call. I can visualize them now, the tiny cabins in which a whole family lived afloat, resplendent in polished brass with roses-and-castles painted utensils, as romantic as any Romany caravan but masking a hard life. During the 1950s I interviewed a man who had been born on such a boat on the Shropshire Canal and had only 'took to the banks', as he put it, to allow his children to go to school. Despite the hardships of canal life, it was a matter of regret that, albeit for the best of reasons, he had taken a job ashore.

As we have seen, the era of canal-building in the Black Country lasted from the late 1760s to the 1850s, and it is somewhat surprising to find that, at least as far as this region is concerned, the golden age of stagecoaching, Christmas-card style, occurred after the building of the main canals – Walsall excepted, which did not boast a canal until 1794. The fact is that turnpiking failed to improve roads to the extent envisaged and it was 1781 before Pickfords advertised a service from Manchester to Birmingham via Wolverhampton and Wednesbury. A few years later the Post Office began national operation of mail coach services, and their Birmingham-Liverpool, Bristol-Manchester coaches passed through the Black Country. In addition to Wolverhampton, Walsall and Dudley became principle staging centres, and most of the region was served by coaches passing through or by local proprietors.

Accidents were frequent well into the nineteenth century. To quote two examples, *The Greyhound*, travelling between Birmingham and Wolverhampton in September 1829, broke an axle and overturned, killing one person and injuring four others, whilst in 1834 *The Albion* was involved in an accident at Walsall when carrying convicts to Portland. The deputy governor was killed and the convicts escaped, helped free of their fetters by sympathetic locals.

Very soon, however, both canal and road traffic was to take a beating, and local people who in the late 1820s may have scoffed at rumours of a fire engine that ran on rails had only to journey to Pensnett to see it for themsevles. Here was one of the world's first industrial steam railways, built to link the mines of Pensnett Chase with the Staffs and Worcs Canal at a convenient point – Ashwood, now a marina. Known officially as the Kingswinford (some would say the Shut End) Railway, it was opened on 2 June 1829. The occasion, fully reported in *Aris's Birmingham Gazette*, conveys the feeling of excitement and wonder that prevailed 'among an immense concourse of spectators from the surrounding country'.

The locomotive operated between two inclined planes and was attached to a train of eight wagons containing some 360 passengers which it conveyed a distance of $3\frac{3}{4}$ miles in half an hour, 'preceded by a band of music'. On a second run twelve carriages of coal were added and, in addition to the 360 official passengers, 'A surging crowd of people swarmed over the coal and wagons, and even into the engine and tender, 340 securing seats on the coal, 20 standing in the tender, while no less than 300 more were carried along clinging to any portion of the vehicle where foothold could be obtained. With this load of some 130 tons, a speed of $3\frac{1}{2}$ miles her pour was obtained.' This now famous locomotive, *The Agenoria* – named after the goddess of courage and industry – worked on this mineral line for about thirty years. It was presented to the South Kensington Museum in 1885 and is today a prime exhibit at the National Railway Museum, York, a solid tribute to Black Country enterprise.

Within a decade the 'awesome' achievement of *The Agenoria* paled into insignificance for, as has been stated, the Grand Junction Railway came from the north in 1837 and in the following year this line was supported by an independently published guide which included a section on what it called the Staffordshire Mining District. Dudley was described as smoky and dirty, Wednesbury as a dark, dirty, mean-looking place, 'The population scarcely ever thinking of anything but eating and drinking when the day's labour is done'. Darlaston was described as 'from a distance looks very well', whilst at Walsall 'The people are certainly more civilised.' Hardly anywhere on the eastern side of the ridge escaped attention: 'The whole district here is a mass of apparent disorganisation and ruin.' Since most of the places mentioned would only be glimpsed on the skyline by anyone travelling this line, it was hardly a good public relations exercise.

By that time the railway boom was endemic right across the country, and railways were being proposed at a great rate by groups of businessmen anxious to get in on the act. Fortunately, not all were built. As it was, the Oxford, Worcester and Wolverhampton crept rather painfully across the region from Stourbridge to Wolverhampton between 1852 and 1854. Quickly named 'the Old Wuss and Wuss' (worse and worse) it reminds one that railways have always been subject to derogatory nicknames. Up to nationalization in 1948, the Great Western and the London, Midland & Scottish were the survivors as far as the Black Country was concerned, and the GWR was 'the Greatest Way Round', whilst the LMS was the 'Lose 'em, Mix 'em and Smash 'em' – a reference to their allegedly careless handling of goods.

The undignified fight for railway proprietorship resulted not only in protracted legal battles but in physical battles on the lines. On 12 and 13 July 1850 fighting occurred when the Shrewsbury-Birmingham Railway Company tried to lay a temporary rail to a nearby canal, the course of which had been altered to permit construction of the Stour Valley Railway. Contractors of this company refused to let the Shrewsbury-Birmingham company's workmen cross their land, and the mayor of Wolverhampton was called to read the Riot Act. However, on 1 December 1851 the Shrewsbury-Birmingham company tried to enforce the running powers, granted by Parliament over the lines of the Stour Valley Company (by this time the London North Western Railway Company), and the latter promptly blocked the line with an engine. The mayor and chief constable arrived with troops, the engineer of the offending company and the engine driver being charged with obstructing an engine and carriage belonging to a rival company. Such incidents underline the fierce competition prevailing.

Throughout the early period of railway expansion, railway companies sought to buy up canals in order to capture their trade, whilst canal proprietors, seeing the writing on the wall and probably speculating in railways themselves, were supposedly equally anxious to get rid of them. It was, as we would say today, a right ball of knitting! But, before leaving this brief comment on steam railway development, it is worth mentioning that anyone wishing to see the Black Country at its most unedifying has only to travel by rail between Birmingham and Wolverhampton or between Birmingham and Stourbridge and look out upon desolate areas of waste land, factory yards with metal scrap and rusting boilers and, perhaps more revealing, all the paraphernalia of urban living in what passes for back gardens: air-raid shelters converted into sheds, crude pigeon lofts, discarded domestic utensils, remnants of prams and cycles, offsetting the brave efforts of those who maintain gardens worthy of the name. As recently as July 1984 the Wolverhampton-Birmingham line was described in the Press as 'the worst view from a train window in Britain'.

To revert to the nineteenth century, extensive development in road, canal and rail transport in itself reflects the importance of the region, and in the hundred years since John Wilkinson appeared on the scene it had changed out of all recognition. Consider population growth based on census returns from 1801, which modern historians consider to be plus or minus ten per cent accurate. Between 1801 and 1811 the population of the Black Country rose from around 97,000 to 129,000; by 1821 the figures had zoomed to over 205,000 and by 1831 to over 450,000. Such dramatic increases could not be absorbed without disaster, especially as they varied from district to district, being largest in

the mining areas. Add to this influx the fact that there were no
controls on building development, no sanitation or health
considerations, and it is hardly surprising that trouble lay in
store. It came in 1832.

Actually, 1832 was a good and bad year. The good was the
passing of the 'great' Reform Bill which, although it did not
enfranchise the working man, was at least a start in the right
direction and widely acclaimed by its advocates. The other
event, far more serious and closer to hand, was an outbreak of
cholera. Bilston, where blame was laid for its appearance in the
region, logged 692 victims plus a further 49 'omitted in the
registers and buried in other parishes'. Tipton sustained 404
deaths of which twelve out of one family of fourteen died, whilst
at Dudley a notice was issued on 1 September to the effect that
the town's churchyards were full and that victims were to be
taken to Netherton churchyard.

Although these figures vary somewhat in different reports,
they convey the extent of the disease which was not of course
confined solely to the Black Country. It did result in a
consideration of health matters particularly in regard to the
provision of a water supply, and two years later Dudley's first
Waterworks Act enabled the pumping of water to two reservoirs.
The year 1835 marked the passing of the Municipal Reform Act,
and this led to the demolition of some slum property. A year
earlier a Poor Law Amendment Act came into being, no doubt
based on the concept that the poorer people created the biggest
health hazard. As a result parishes were grouped into Unions,
and I recall that as late as the Depression of the 1930s fear of the
Union, or workhouse, was strong among older people.

Despite these progressive moves, more necessary in the Black
Country than anywhere else in the country at the time, it was not
until 1848 that the Public Health Act compelled local authorities
to appoint medical officers of health and attempt to deal with
the problems of a heavily industrialized environment. Ironically,
cholera paid a return visit in the following year!

Thanks to two important reports commissioned in the early
1840s – the Children's Employment Commission Report and the
Midland Mining Commission Report – there is a wealth of
information on the life and times of the population.
Representatives of all sections of the Black Country community

were interviewed: children, working men and women, employers, magistrates, the clergy, Sunday school teachers, police constables and surgeons, and from their comments one learns on the one hand of severe cruelty to boys in the lock trade at Willenhall (said to have been drawn upon by Disraeli in his novel *Sybil*), and on the other that in some pits prayers were said and swearing was not permitted.

Children went into the coalfields at the age of seven or eight, and many had experienced an accident before even reaching that age. In small, under-capitalized pits we are told that little children were sent into holes in the mines with baskets to get coals, bringing them to the foot of the shaft by dragging them along on hands and knees. Again, boys of twelve or thirteen, 'naked almost to the navel', were urging laden carts forward on 'narrow pigmian railways ... they laid their hands on the hinder parts of the cart and stretched out with their feet far behind, their heads hardly within two feet of the ground, they ferreted onward ...' It is a shameful record, but Black Country people still retain a fierce pride in the fact that there is no record of women or girls being employed underground in the region. Whilst this may be thought to be clutching at a straw, the point is made again and again whenever the nineteenth-century iniquities come under discussion.

Pit-bank wenches there were aplenty, a different thing altogether, 'standing on the banks near the mouth of the shaft and, when a skip comes up, they unhook it and empty the coals'. It was found by the Commissioner that, 'The girls are generally singing at their work and always appear smiling and cheerful.' Well, maybe: but *always* would have meant the few minutes that the officials were on the scene.

Overall, despite sparing no punches in including stories of cruelty and hardship where they saw it, the Commissioners tended to stress the positive side. Hence those pit-bank wenches were reported as 'possessing a physical vigor far surpassing that of young women brought up in the clear air of great towns'. In like vein, 'The children employed in the mines of the South Staffordshire coalfield are in a very far superior condition as regards wages and all the necessary comforts of life wherever wages can procure, to the children of the manufacturing districts.' This was a question of degree and it was apparent that on the whole children working in the mines were treated better than most of those apprenticed to a trade. Perhaps that is why the Commissioners were able to report that, 'There are almost no boys in the union workhouses at Walsall, Wolverhampton, Dudley and Stourbridge, and there is no schoolmaster at any of these establishments.' They were shocked at the lack of education. How could anyone not have heard of London and Queen Victoria! So whilst there are aspects of the reports that are contradictory and puzzling to us now, they did alert the government to some of the iniquitous practices of the time, none of which was more damaging to the working class than the tommy system, by which wages were paid in goods sold at shops owned by middlemen, butty colliers in the case of collieries, and factors or foggers in the nail trade.

Nailors were by far the most exploited victims of trucking as it was called, and nowhere is their plight more vividly portrayed than in a novel *A Capful O' Nails* written in 1896 by David Christie Murray, a native of West Bromwich, based on recollections of his childhood. Nailmaking had been a cottage industry since the sixteenth century particularly in Dudley, Sedgley, Rowley Regis and Halesowen areas, often commencing as a sideline to supplement income from farming, but the tommy shop system was a blight of the nineteenth century. Murray describes how a nailor dares to challenge a fogger who is cheating him twice, once when selling him iron to make the nails and again when buying back the finished nails, each time using false weights, of which he had three sets: a light set to sell with, a heavy set to buy with and another set to show the inspector. Not content with that form of deceit, the fogger maintained a shop at which the nailmaking families were intimidated into buying inferior food at high prices.

The defiant nailor in the novel said that the foggers were forbidden by law to keep a tommy shop: 'But there ain't a fogger in the country who hasn't got a relative in that line of business. We're forced to buy bad and dear, or woe betide us.' There was the nub of it, for an Anti Truck Bill of 1831 (the result of a private Bill introduced by Edward Littleton whom we have met before and who became Lord Hatherton in 1835) was largely ineffective, and in 1870 a Commission was set up to see what could be done. At a meeting of the Horsenail Forgers' and Common Nail

Forgers' Association in October 1882, it was said that trucking was on the increase, and a resolution was passed to form a National Anti-Truck League. Even so, it was not until 1887 that the Truck Amendment Act was passed and the system brought gradually to an end – a good fifty years after Littleton's attempt to stamp it out!

Any serious attempt to improve social conditions in the 1840s was doomed to failure by reason of continued growth in population and intensification in the iron trade which reached a peak of production in the early 1850s despite a slight recession in 1847 when the railway building boon dipped sharply. This hiccup did not deter Lord Ward (he became Earl of Dudley in 1860) opening a large new ironworks at Round Oak, Brierley Hill, in 1857. After all, there had always been ups and downs in the trade, notably in 1816 following the end of the French wars, and there would be others, despite which, as we shall see, the Round Oak works was to survive through to the 1970s as one of the most significant of all Black Country steelworks. Note the word 'steel', for in general the introduction in 1856 of the Bessemer process for making mild steel hastened the decline of the wrought-iron industry, but no Black Country ironmaster saw any need to change over to it for a vital eight years – an unusual lack of foresight.

Other warning signs were even more ominous. By 1860 the coal and iron-ore resources had begun to give out, and as the number of mines decreased, with consequently fewer pumping engines at work, pit flooding became more prevalent. In 1873, when the South Staffs Mines Drainage Act was passed, it was estimated that twenty million tons of coal and one million tons of iron ore were under water. This, despite earlier attempts, specifically at Tipton when local coalmasters agreed to share the cost of pumping out their mines instead of each trying to cope individually, and again when the Old Hill Mines Drainage Company attempted the same thing on a bigger scale in 1870. Alas, even the Act of 1873, with its power to levy a rate on coal, iron ore and fireclay mined in the area to pay for pumping operations, ultimately failed. The problem was simply too great, and according to Raybould in his *Economic Emergence of The Black Country* some forty million tons of coal was waterlogged by 1900.

Happily for the region a host of new industries had arisen long before the mineral wealth vanished, keeping the Black Country to the forefront with a finger virtually in every manufacturing pie and exporting throughout the world. This industrial pre-eminence was underlined at the Great Exhibition of 1851, when Black Country firms supplied the structural ironwork and glass for the Crystal Palace as well as numerous exhibits, including a piece of coal from Tipton which is said to have weighed six tons and measured six feet high by eighteen inches diameter. Various developments in a multitude of industries have been left for later chapters. Suffice to say that by the latter part of the nineteenth century a tremendous diversity of new skills and crafts was learned and opportunities were grasped, so that surely nowhere else in the world was so much happening in so confined an area.

At the same time piped water, gas lighting, hospitals and Ragged Schools, museums, art galleries, mechanics' institutes and free libraries were established to improve the lot of the people, music halls came to provide entertainment and respite from toil and poverty, and the Salvation Army and Temperance Movement came to counter excessive drunkenness and moral degradation. In 1866 no fewer than fifty-five public houses were noted as serving one small locality of six thousand people! The Black Country has always had more than its fair share of public houses. It is no laughing matter but during World War II, whilst there was no saturation bombing of the region, many of Hitler's bombs fell on licensed premises – they were difficult to miss! An opening at the top of High Street, Dudley, opposite St Thomas' Church, was the site of the Three Swans until it was destroyed by a bomb in 1940. The church still bears the scars of damaged stonework.

As for improved transportation, in 1872 the first horse-drawn tram ran in the region, the steam tram arrived in 1883, and ten years later the electric tram appeared, building up to a remarkable transport system which by the 1920s deposited workpeople virtually at the gates of all the major factories. By the end of the century Black Country men had made their first motor car and all in all were nicely poised for a grand new order of progress in what was to prove the twilight of the old Europe.

Throughout the long period under discussion in this chapter, strikes, lockouts and accidents at work were commonplace.

Often industrial and political unrest was severe, protracted and violent, whilst religion – particularly Methodism – had a role to play through decades of hardship and deprivation for working people who, even if relatively well paid betimes, had little inherent sense of providence and husbandry. Black Country people are rooted in their past even when they have moved away, and to visit the Black Country Museum is for most pensioners not to see something archaic but to be reintroduced to things they had been compelled to tolerate and glad to get rid of: washing mangle and dolly tub, flat-iron and black-leaded grate, red-tiled floor and shared outside lavatory.

Thus far I have attempted to give an overall picture of a region of great vitality moving forward into the twentieth century. Now the objective is to move from the general to the particular, pinpointing events in specific areas and coming up to the present day, bearing in mind that the Black Country was born not as one area but as a collection of separate entities of often fierce independence brought together on and about a unique coalfield, heaven-sent complete with an abundance of ironstone, limestone and clay to give a long summer of unrivalled importance.

4

Dudley

It is said that whichever way you approach Dudley you have to climb, but whilst it may appear so, it is not quite the case, for when approaching along the ridge from Sedgley the undulations are slight. Similarly, arriving from the Birmingham side along the ridge through Rowley Regis, there is actually a drop into Dudley town. Nevertheless, it is all high ground ranging between five and eight hundred feet.

Another well-aired saying that it is a top-coat colder than Stourbridge has more truth. There is a place on the ridge called Highland Road, Shavers End, where I lived for a time, and the late Norman Pett, artist and creator of 'Jane' in the *Daily Mirror*, drew for me a cartoon of the address depicting a Scottish Highlander cutting his throat with a razor. In fact Shavers End is thought to be so called because the wind is keen enough to shave one, and it certainly does blow – right off the Bristol Channel, as locals boast. Well, there's nothing to stop it! In Black Country parlance: 'It dow stop ter goo round yer, it goes through yer.'

The natural starting point for a close look at Dudley must be the castle, already mentioned but worthy of more detailed attention. Alas, it no longer belongs to the town, which is possibly why, for all it presents an impressive backdrop, local people scarcely give it a glance as they go about their business. It's always been there and that's it! But when I was a lad in the 1920s, and for decades earlier, the castle and its tree-covered grounds lay open to the public. It was possible to roam amid the ruins and dream one's dreams of bygone times when, to quote an account of the last great ball held there before the fire of 1750, 'The courtyard was littered with splendid equipages, sounding with the rattling of wheels and the voices of coachmen and grooms and blazing with light from every window ... the sounds of many voices, harps and violins, issuing from every doorway.' Also, as late as the 1930s it was possible to stroll the lovers' walks around the lower slopes of the hill from the Tipton end to an opening close to the present cinema on Castle Hill, a steep main road into the town.

From the 1850s the castle was an important recreational venue, and the annual three-day Whitsuntide fête was a major event in the local calendar. A 1916 account states that tramways operating from Birmingham and other districts made special arrangements for large numbers of visitors and that teas would be provided at a cottage within the grounds. As many as twenty thousand people visited on a single day and at that time one could ascend the summit of the castle keep, from which it was possible on a clear day to see, not forever, but parts of the counties of Worcester, Stafford, Derby, Leicester, Warwick, Salop and Hereford and parts of Wales. The keep is the most distantly visible part of the ruins, and a writer described having paid a penny to go to the top, where he purchased a small stone, rather implying that it was being sold off in bits.

The fêtes died out after the 1914-18 war but the grounds remained open, and at one time it was the understood thing for girls to go skipping in the castle courtyard on Good Fridays. However, in 1937 a zoo was opened in the grounds, and although it has suffered various financial crises and change of ownership, it is today a premier attraction. At the outset the zoo was considered to be unique because the animals were not caged but placed in enclosures, making imaginative use of the lie of the land and concrete surfaces. The turnstiled entrance, not widely acclaimed at the time, is now 'listed' as an early example of concrete architecture.

The zoo is currently managed by a trust which is a registered charity, and many firms and individuals adopt and sponsor specific animals, an arrangement that has worked successfully since 1978. It is sad that, despite all the zoo has to offer, the castle is not freely accessible to the public, but such loss has to be set against the fact that the trust has accepted responsibility for the restoration of the castle ruins and much valuable work has been carried out. One of the most important features is a triple gateway, twenty-seven feet long by seventeen wide, of two storeys, having twelfth-century side walls six inches thick. Within the remains of the curtain wall can be seen the layout of the hall, chapel, kitchen and other buildings. An archaeological project was started in 1983 to carry out excavations to seek evidence of a castle on the site prior to the present structure, and finds within the first year include fragments of Saxon pottery, ancient coins and relics such as domestic utensils dating from the Civil War. A full excavation could last well into the 1990s. Still a feature of the castle are two guns captured during the Crimean War at Sebastopol. In 1857 some joker fired one of them, as a result of which they were spiked to prevent a repetition of the incident.

Natural progression from the castle takes us to nearby Priory Park, where the medieval remains, largely of local limestone, are neatly kept. From 1825 these ruins were contained within the private grounds of a hall which still stands, built by the Earl of Dudley as a residence for his mining agent, but today the ruins form part of a public park on the Priory Estate. This large housing estate on land purchased from Lord Dudley in the late 1920s was heralded as being responsible for preventing Dudley's continuing as a 'slum ridden town, with little or no chance of improving the standard of the people'. I recall the area as consisting of farms, cornfields, lanes and ponds, still no doubt much as they were in the days of the 'black monks' so called by reason of their black habit and cowl.

The Priory Estate extends almost to the foot of the Wren's Nest Hill where the entrance to limestone caverns has long been fenced off for safety. The Wren's Nest is a seventy-four-acre national nature reserve on which a geographical trail has been laid out with bollards. In fact, there are really two trails, one for the inexperienced and another for those possessing some knowledge of geology. A booklet is available giving a virtually step-by-step guide to what is potentially dangerous ground. Although fossils may still be found, the hill has been well combed by generations of hopefuls, and hammering at the rock face in search of specimens is discouraged. In the middle of the

Dudley Castle – view from Kate's Hill 1849

The Priory Ruins, Dudley, 'about a bow shoot westward of the castle'

Dudley market place with its impressive fountain dating to 1867

Black Country Museum Village. The Bottle and Glass public house (left) faces the chapel

A sixteenth-century building in Victoria Street, Wolverhampton, restored during 1979–81

ST. PET

St Peter's Church, Wolverhampton

Right: St Matthew's Church on its limestone hill high above Walsall tow

Town Hall, Bilston with the dome of St Leonard's Church peeping over the roof

Equestrian statue to Prince Albert, unveiled by Queen Victoria in 1866, Queen Square, Wolverhampton

Entrance to Walsall Arboretum

The Oak House, West Bromwich

Queen Victoria passes through a triumphal arch of coal at the railway station, Wolverhampton. The occasion was to unveil a statue to Prince Albert c.1866

last century three fossil shops existed in the town, and callers bought, sold or exchanged specimens rather as one might deal in postage stamps today. It is not entirely fanciful to imagine prospectors hoping to strike it rich in a gold-rush style scramble, but in fact fossils were abundant and, as already stated, found their way to the world's museums. Limepit Lane, Dudley, leads from Shavers End to the Wren's Nest, a reminder of the quarrying carried out to a declining extent until 1924. Hereabouts Abraham Darby was born of a Quaker family, growing up to make industrial history at Coalbrookdale. Few people realize that he was a Black Country man, but it would be difficult now to know precisely on the Wrenner, as locals call the Wren's Nest, where to place a commemorative plaque.

Descendants of Fitz Ansculf who possessed Dudley at the time of Domesday were named Pagnel, and one Gervase Pagnel gave a charter to found the priory. It is fitting that near the ruins are two parallel residential roads, Gervase Drive and Pagnel Drive, providing a modern link with the twelfth century. The charter included the churches of St Edmund and St Thomas. The former, probably of Saxon origin, was demolished during the Civil War, not as might be supposed by the attacking Roundheads but by Royalist defenders of the castle who did not want anything standing nearby which could afford shelter to the enemy. It was not rebuilt until 1724, and meanwhile its parish was combined with that of St Thomas, an unusual procedure. Old St Thomas' Church was demolished in 1816 and a new church opened two years later. These churches stand at opposite ends of the town, and the main street developed between them. St Edmund's is known locally as Lower Church (although considered 'high', being Anglo-Catholic) and St Thomas' is known as Top Church, its tall spire standing out on the skyline for over a dozen miles to the west, a landmark for generations until dwarfed by three towerblocks of flats built in the 1960s.

Apart from a small cluster of buildings huddled at the foot of the castle, Dudley grew so slowly along the hilly road between the churches that a man writing in 1904 about the days of his youth said: 'For many years of my life there were only two churches in Dudley, St Edmund's and St Thomas.' He would have seen more later, beginning with St James' at Eve Hill and St John's at Kate's Hill, almost identical. It is often thought that

St James' is of an earlier date, whereas in fact the original St James' was the medieval priory chapel itself.

Who was Eve who gave her name to a hill on the ridge as well as to a lane a mile further out towards Sedgley? And did the children in the little church school there chant 'Deliver us from eve 'ill'? – aspirates not being a strong feature of local speech. And who was Kate who gave her name to Kate's Hill? We do not know, but the distaff side seems to have been favoured, for although Black Country men, particularly in the nineteenth century, had a reputation as wife-thumpers, there are several cases of womenfolk being favoured with recognition. For example the brewery firm of Julia Hanson & Son, founded in 1847, had the distinction of being the only brewery in the country with a lady's name. Its trademark was Dudley Castle before it became part of a large brewery company in 1943. Brewing is still carried out at Hanson's within sight and smell of Top Church! Conversely there were incidents of so-called wife selling. In 1859 hundreds of people congregated to witness such an exhibition, the first bid being a halfpenny rising to 6 pence (6d.), at which point the woman was declared sold. This practice was not as bad as it appears, being a mutual rough-and-ready system of divorce satisfactory to most parties. Well, so we are told now!

The town has a wide market-place on a level stretch of the main street, now a precincted area. It was not always wide, for the first town hall stood there, a narrow two-storey building with an arch through the centre and a clocktower on the roof. It formed part of what was known as Middle Row and was demolished in 1860, leaving a large area approximate to that of today where market stalls form soldierly lines and replica nineteenth-century footpath posts serve as ornamental features. A new town hall was erected in Priory Street, and one may as well follow it there to look at the complex of public buildings that have welded themselves into a block as if for mutual support. What remains of the 1860s town hall, which served for a time as a police station, is a strange building for the Victorians to have erected, not as a folly but for municipal use, for it has castellated towers, a mock barbican gateway and slits in the walls through which boiling oil could be poured, presumably upon complaining ratepayers!

Abutting this building and extending round the corner into St James' Road is the present town hall, opened in 1928 and incorporating law courts, war memorial, banqueting hall and, by 1931, the Brooke Robinson Museum. Robinson was much revered in his time. Born in 1836, he became a solicitor, then county coroner and subsequently the town's MP for twenty years. He was an avid collector of all kinds of historic items and left provision in his will for the erection of a museum named after him. The trust took up the matter with the Charity Commissioners and town council, and it was agreed that the legacy should be used to assist in the provision of a town hall which should bear the name of Brooke Robinson and that the new buildings should contain a room set apart as a museum to house his collection. So Dudley got its third town hall, but the room 'set apart' proved difficult to supervise and was often closed, a state of affairs rectified somewhat belatedly in 1979 when the collection was transferred over the road to the art gallery.

The war memorial chamber, with its entrance below a seventy-foot clocktower, is worthy of inspection. Cut into the stone are the words

> If you think, have a kindly thought,
> If you speak, speak generously,
> Of those who as heroes fought
> And died to keep you free.

Below the town hall in St James' Road is the public library, mecca of my childhood days when I could hardly wait to get a 'grown-up' borrower's ticket. Opened in 1909, the building remains in my memory as the place where my unemployed father, like so many of his contemporaries in the 1930s, whiled away his time in the reading-room looking at newspapers from which diligent librarians had snipped the racing news to discourage gambling. The building was altered and extended in 1966.

Completing the complex is the council house, opened in 1935, with civic gardens on the opposite side of Priory Road, where stands a statue of Apollo and, in the distance, nestling against the wooded slopes of the castle grounds, the technical college's modern profile is in sharp contrast to the priory ruins nearby. On the opposite side of St James' Road to the town hall stands the art gallery, opened in 1884 as both a free library and school of art although no work of art was acquired until two years later. Now the central museum and art gallery, it is well utilized and supported with exhibitions covering a wide range of interests. Here are the Brooke Robinson Museum and a geographical gallery outlining the town's fossil heritage, although by no means all the specimens in stock can be displayed. A report in 1984 claimed that around ten thousand fossils dating back some 400 million years were stored in cellars in less than ideal conditions.

Placed on the wall outside the art gallery is a set of meteorological instruments consisting of temperature, barometer and wind-speed gauges which, although on a prominent corner position, are rarely noted by passers-by. An inscription reveals that they were presented by James Smellie (mayor 1924-5) in memory of his wife, Ann Grace Smellie, mayoress of Dudley from 10 November 1924 to 14 April 1926. These instruments look over a large cobbled square which serves as a car-park and a turning area for buses to Wolverhampton. This is the Stone Street site of the Dudley Flint Glassworks dating to 1766. Strange to reflect that on this uninspiring spot were made some of the world's finest glass, that gold enamelling was perfected here and that a gold enamelled dessert service 'furnished to the Corporation of London, on Her Majesty Queen Victoria's first visit to the Guildhall on 9 November 1837' was manufactured. The firm had ceased to operate by 1841, and the building was used for a variety of purposes until it became unsafe and was demolished in 1886, after which the site became a vegetable market.

If plans for the redevelopment of this area come to fruition, the next few years will see drastic changes in Stone Street. Not that they are likely to result in the loss of the Saracen's Head hotel which stands here on the site of a former inn and has in its time played an important part in the social and political life of the town, though rather less so than the Dudley Arms hotel in the market-place, demolished in 1970. There had been a pub on the latter site since Queen Anne's time, and it became a main coaching inn as well as the chief focal point for the town's bigwigs. Brooke Robinson thanked his cheering election supporters from an upper window there in days when politicians attracted vociferous attention and were not the two-dimensional characters of a television screen. The Court Leet met there, and in more recent times the Prince of Wales, later Edward VIII, is said to have visited incognito following a visit to a cinema when a guest of the Earl of Dudley at Himley Hall. How sad that its prime site fell to supermarket barons!

One can return from Stone Street to the market-place via the Fountain Arcade (c. 1925) which brings us to the fountain itself, sometimes referred to affectionately as 'the spout'. Sculpted by James Forsyth, it was considered splendid enough to be exhibited at the Paris exhibition of 1867 before being installed at Dudley and unveiled by Georgina, Countess of Dudley, in October of the same year, 'the property of the people of Dudley for ever'. It is there still, despite attempts to move it into a park out of the way of traffic, no longer a problem since pedestrianization. Although the fountain has suffered periods of neglect, it remains a notable feature, water flowing from the mouth of its marine horses, dolphins and lions, into large horse-and cattle-basins.

Leading off the market-place on the opposite side to the civic complex is Churchill Precinct, following the line of what used to be Hall Street. Here one of the town's modern treasures can be seen, the Churchill commemorative screen stretching the width of a side arm of the precinct and showing in painted glass illustrations of the war leader surrounded by associated planes, ships, tanks and so forth. By its very nature it is vulnerable to vandalism and, like the Britain it depicts, is somewhat battered. In concept it is a splendid piece of work, and one can only hope it will remain at least more or less intact. Here too can be found a valuable asset to the town in the form of an information centre, far superior to the norm and equipped to offer the visitor courteous help and advice.

As to the town centre shopping facilities in general, it has to be said that whilst virtually all the internationally known stores are present, the 1980s has seen a decline in the better-class establishments in favour of cut-price enterprises. The former Co-op store (grandly dubbed 'the emporium') has become a mini-market, whilst next door a drapery store of distinction closed after more than a hundred years of trading.

Dudley is short on statues, the 2nd Earl of Dudley being the sole real-life beneficiary. His statue stands on a traffic island outside the castle grounds entrance of pre-zoo days and was

erected by public subscription in 1888, 'in great remembrance of
the many benefits conferred by him upon this town and district'.
Such a sentiment is at odds with those of some present-day
historians who blame the nineteenth-century lords for gross –
some go so far as to say murderous – exploitation of working
people in the pursuit of their mineral wealth. Or course the
Dudley lords were all-powerful, of course they exploited, but it
seems pointless to place on their worm-eaten shoulders the social
conscience of more enlightened times. In fact, they did 'put
something back', for all over the region one finds evidence of
their contributions to church-building and other causes. For
example, the Guest Hospital in Tipton Road was founded
originally in 1859 as an asylum for those who had lost their
eyesight whilst working in his lordship's coalpits and limestone
quarries. It consisted of twenty-six cottages built of sandstone,
and on the opening day Dudley was *en fête*, bands patrolling the
streets and five oxen slaughtered 'to provide joints of beef for the
indigent poor of the town'. Further amenities were to be added,
but alas for good intentions the project failed because the
sufferers for whom it was intended stubbornly refused to be
separated from their families to reside in an area a good half
mile from the town centre. As a result the asylum remained
unoccupied until the trustees of a prosperous nail- and
chain-manufacturer and merchant, Joseph Guest, suggested to
the Earl that some of the Guest money could be made available
to convert the building to a hospital. The Earl agreed and the
resultant Guest Hospital was opened in 1871, enlarged over the
years to serve as the town's chief hospital until 1984 when a
brand-new hospital, built on an area of dereliction, was opened
and christened Russells Hall Hospital.

Russells Hall is an old name that has re-emerged at Dudley,
for although the original hall, situated about a mile from the new
hospital, was demolished in 1844, Russell family links have been
traced to the thirteenth century. Between the old hall and
hospital lies a part of the Russell Hall estate known to me as a
boy as the Old Park, a waste area then considered unsafe because
of 'crownings-in' (subsidence due to mine workings) and also
because of underground fires. Yet today's Russells Hall estate
covers all but a small part of the area with no major difficulties
so far as I am aware, such is the expertise in modern building.

Just as Dudley never had a canal save for the legging tunnel beneath it, so it did not have a main-line railway station, being linked to the Birmingham-Wolverhampton main line (electrified since the 1960s) by what was known as 'the Dudley Dodger', a train which shuttled passengers to Dudley Port. However, Dudley lost both passenger service and goods depot despite attempts to save it from closure, and in 1967 the station site was transformed into one of Britain's new freightline terminals, which it still is. Walking from this terminal up Castle Hill towards the town, one passes the one-time entertainment centre, of which only a cinema remains. The plush Odeon of my youth is an assembly hall for Jehovah's Witnesses, and the Hippodrome immediately opposite is a bingo hall. What memories that theatre holds for me, seated in the audience on the Friday night of the opening week, December 1938. Why Friday? Because Jack Hylton and his band were broadcasting live during the performance, and radio was the new miracle of the provinces despite the fact that by then London was experimenting with television. Designated a number-one variety house, the Hippodrome brought to Dudley the major performers of the 1940s and 50s: all gone now save the sad, lonely building. It replaced Dudley's first real theatre, the Opera House, opened in 1899 with a performance of *The Mikado* by the D'Oyly Carte Opera Company and built through the enterprise of a local man, John Clements, for years a leading light in the town's Garrick Club. He was duly praised for 'providing a magnificent and commodious theatre and catering for intellectural enjoyment'. I like the 'intellectural' bit, for indeed it is necessary to emphasize that the Black Country was not a hundred per cent cultural desert, as it is often thought to be even today. The Opera House was a permanent venue for theatre-goers for thirty-seven years, only to be gutted by fire on a Sunday morning in 1936 between the outgoing scenery of one show and the incoming scenery of another.

Next to the surviving cinema is the zoo, completing the leisure/entertainment facilities at Castle Hill. But if one heads in the opposite direction, past the freightline terminal and across Tipton Road, the Sports Centre is reached with its county cricket ground and football pitch. Note 'county cricket', for here the Worcestershire County Cricket Club have played fixtures for almost a hundred years, a reminder that, until the West Midland County was formed in 1974, Dudley was in Worcestershire, an island within Staffordshire. (Its churches are still in the Worcester diocese.)

One of the first intimations Dudley received that it was to suffer for the limestone extraction of former times occurred at the Sports Centre some years ago when a section of ground collapsed. Then in May 1985 a far more disastrous subsidence occurred at the Centre when a forty-foot diameter hole appeared in the cricket pitch, as a result of which the whole sports complex has been closed temporarily as a safety measure. The eventual cost of making it safe, along with other parts of the borough which are riddled with caverns is expected to run into tens of millions, and central government is already making a contribution. However, the full extent of this problem – which extends to other parts of the Black Country, notably Walsall – is not yet fully diagnosed.

There are few ancient buildings of note in Dudley, but in Wolverhampton Street, standing well back from the building line through an archway, is the Presbyterian, later Unitarian Old Meeting House. The original building was erected in 1702 but was burnt down during the Sacheverell riots of 1715. A grant from Parliament enabled rebuilding in 1717, and in 1869 the interior was 'a great deal altered and renovated'. Their supporter, Dr Joseph Priestley – discoverer of oxygen and the man whose Birmingham home was sacked by a mob because he appeared to support the French Revolution – preached here in 1780 and was present on later occasions. This building is still in use. Incidentally, another link with Dr Priestley and the Black Country is that he married the daughter of Isaac Wilkinson, ironmaster, of Bersham near Wrexham, and it was Isaac's son who came to Bradley, Bilston, in 1757 to found the iron trade in the region.

Also in Wolverhampton Street, much more prominent and imposing, is Finch House, a two-storey building now used for commercial purposes, the front of which bears the date 1707 and the initials of Joseph and Mary Finch. This family has been traced to the sixteenth century, and in 1636 one Thomas Finch was a nailor. Running parallel with Wolverhampton Street between the civic centre and St James' Church, Eve Hill, is St James' Road, in the middle of which is Dudley Grammar School, although one cannot now call it that. The present building dates to 1898 and is dismissed by Pevsner in just three words, 'flaming red brick', but the school was founded in 1526.

Mineral extraction excepted, Dudley is not noted for any specific trade or industry as are most Black Country towns, since it shared nailmaking with surrounding districts, although one can gather from the industrial use to which the priory ruins were put (fender-polishing) that the manufacture of hearth furniture was long established. A directory of 1929 lists eighteen such manufacturers, and a few lingered until coal fires went out of fashion. One eighteenth-century trade did identify with the town, largely in the hands of one man, James Wilkinson – that of anvil- and vice-making. It can be appreciated that these articles were prime requisites in pre-factory days when hundreds of smiths hammered at nails, horseshoes, chains and all kinds of ironwork, and Wilkinson (no relation to the Bradley ironmaster) was certainly in a fair way of business, issuing his own trade tokens in 1812, some of which survive in the hands of collectors. 'We had no carts or wagons to convey our anvils and vices to Birmingham for sale to the factors, but had to travel with them in large baskets slung on horses' backs, and in single file we travelled over Bromwich Heath ... truly a wearisome procedure.' This acount reminds us that road transport was still a major problem despite turnpike trust improvements spread over several decades.

There were a number of glassworks in Dudley in addition to that in Stone Street, originated as offshoots of the more famed and enduring Stourbridge glass industry. We are told that in 1830 there were no fewer than two hundred people working in five Dudley glasshouses, and it is of little purpose to attempt to pinpoint them now. Certainly one was in Downing Street and another at Dixons Green, which is an extension of Hall Street, bringing us nicely to an important part of Dudley's twentieth-century industry, for it was here at the top of Dixons Green that the National Projectile Factory was built to provide munitions in World War I. Commonly called 'the Nash', it was a major employer of labour, male and female, and attracted the attention of zepplins which luckily failed to make a hit. As a boy I heard stories of bombs being dropped on a canal on the Netherton side under the impression that the glistening water was the glass roof of the factory! Memories of 'the Nash' are almost gone as its workers have died off, but the building still stands behind high walls, sub-divided to suit a miscellany of industries.

After the 1914-18 war motor-vehicle manufacture came to Dudley and neighbouring Tipton when J. Harper Bean, son of a former mayor, Sir George Bean, went into partnership with the Hadfield steel company of Sheffield and others to produce cars. Ambitions ran high, and in November 1919 an announcement was made concerning 'a great campaign of mass production under which an initial output of fifty cars a week would build up to two thousand a week by mid-1922.' No high-priced vehicles would be built, and standardization was the aim. Great stuff for the newly unemployed ex-servicemen!

Alas, such hopes were not realized and production lasted only until 1929, but Bean cars are prized by vintage car enthusiasts and they did achieve successes in their day: notably a Bean car was the first automobile to cross the Australian continent, and the cars also enjoyed royal patronage in the 1920s. Commercial Beans also did well in the export field. Strictly, Tipton must share equally with Dudley in the history of this company, although the former head office at Waddams Pool, Dudley, still has the words 'Bean Cars Ltd' cut into the stone as a permanent reminder. As with the nearby 'Nash', several enterprises subsequently occupied the works (demolished in 1984), one in particular being an American company which manufactured the yoyo. Older readers will remember the national yoyo craze of the 1930s – far greater than any craze since, whether hoola-hoop or skateboard.

As to other industries, newspaper reports of the tailoring trade during the 1880s gave the town a bad name by reason of 'blackguardly middlemen and chicken-hearted seamsters', and there were a number of small ironworks making bedsteads. Leaving Netherton aside temporarily, Dudley boasted until the 1920s a major ironworks of distinction, and this was at Woodside about a mile and a half from the town: Cochrane's Ironworks where many of my elders worked and where, in addition to the ironwork for the Crystal Palace, ironwork was made for Westminster Bridge, Cannon Street and Charing Cross Stations among others, as well the Clifton Suspension Bridge and various seaside piers. The company also supplied cast-iron pillarboxes for the GPO, specifically Britain's First National Standard pillarbox introduced in 1859 and those of hexagonal design which replaced them in 1866 and remained standard until 1879. One way or another there is ample evidence of Black Country workmanship still to be found around the country.

Over the years Dudley has produced a number of outstanding personalities in the realms of sport and entertainment, and the one who 'put Dudley on the map', to quote the mayor at the time, was tennis-player Dorothy Round (1909-82). In 1934 she won the Wimbledon women's singles final, beating an American run of success that had lasted since 1927, and in 1937 she won the title again, thus becoming the only British player to win the championship twice since 1927. Moreover, partnered by a Japanese player in 1934 and by Fred Perry in 1935 and '36, she was three times a mixed doubles winner. Dudley folk loved 'Our Dorothy' as they called her, and in 1938, when she married a local doctor and became Mrs Little, it was a gala occasion and children were given a half-day holiday. 'I had no idea the wedding would cause so much attention,' she recalled. 'The streets were crowded.' No other British girl has since won Wimbledon twice, yet outside the Black Country she is almost forgotten.

Another sporting character, barely a year old when Dorothy Round took her title a second time, was Duncan Edwards, the Manchester United footballer who was among those who died as a result of the Munich air disaster in February 1958, when he was twenty-one years of age. A pupil of Wolverhampton Street Schools, Dudley, he became England Schoolboy Captain in 1952 and made his league début for Manchester United in April 1953. Two years later he became the youngest player to gain an England cap and was to play eighteen times for his country. He is buried in Dudley's 'new' cemetery under a headstone which has an engraved picture of him holding a ball above his head for a throw-in. Soccer fans still make pilgrimage to his grave and there are stained glass windows to his memory in St Francis' Church on the Priory Estate close to where he lived.

Dudley's contribution to the entertainment profession includes Clarkson Rose (1891-1968) who went on the stage at the age of eighteen and in 1921 began his renowned 'Twinkle' seaside revues. Billy Russell (1893-1971), although actually born in

Birmingham, grew up in Dudley and sold programmes at the then Empire Theatre in Hall Street when it was opened by Dan Leno in 1903. This theatre had a short life as a music hall, became a cinema and has long since been demolished, but Billy Russell became hooked on the stage and became a great exponent of Black Country humour, billing himself 'On Behalf of the Working Classes' and sporting a walrus moustache and smoking a clay pipe. He said he never had a gag-writer for there was material all around: 'See a boxer with bow legs ... That's so's they cor knock 'im over!'

Mr Russell, to give him his Sunday name, had a serious side and having travelled the world declared that nowhere had he seen slums to equal those of Dudley in the early years of this century, referring in particular to Birmingham Street, Oakeywell Street, Fisher Street and Flood Street. In this he was echoing a report of 1851, when a government inspector proclaimed the town as being the unhealthiest in the country. One child in five died under the age of twelve months, and only about three babies in every ten would reach the age of maturity. 'That was in Queen Victoria's sixty glorious years,' Billy Russell wrote. 'Sixty *cruel* years.' Apparently little had changed in the seventy or so years between those two statements. However, if Dudley was backward, it has made up for it since, and even before the 1939-45 war considerable progress had been made, hundreds of slum-dwellers being moved to new areas, such as the Priory Estate. The specific slum streets named above are now occupied by vast open-air car-parks, and Fisher Street is the site of the bus station.

Dudley is the home of the Black Country Museum, a growing asset which is attracting over 200,000 visitors a year. An open-air museum, it was formally launched in 1975, although individuals and interested organizations had worked towards it for years. For a long time it had the appearance of a building site, for much work has been done on constructing a typical Black Country village street consisting of carefully re-erected buildings from all over the region. A row of cottages came from Old Hill, a chemist shop that had belonged to a certain Emile Doo was moved lock stock and barrel (or pill and powder) from Netherton, and a traditional ironmonger's is based on a shop at Oldbury. The 'village' chapel was formerly the Darby End Providence Church

(Netherton), and close by is the Bottle and Glass pub (licensed) which came from the Wordsley area of Stourbridge, the proximity of chapel and pub affirming the Black Country man's interpretation of 'thirst after righteousness'. The splendid bridge over the canal arm, by which one enters the village, is dated 1879 and came from Wolverhampton, whilst even the restaurant is based on a stable block from Wednesbury. There is the headgear of a colliery, aptly named Racecourse Colliery because from 1837 to 1848 a racecourse existed nearby, a boat-building dock, working rolling mill, chainshop, bakery and much more beside. A tramway runs from the entrance to the 'village' at the terminus of which is a small fairground with traditional rides and, to the delight of conservationists, a market stall area paved with stone setts from Dudley's market-place.

A point of interest is that the houses have coal fires, and special permission has had to be obtained to set aside the Clean Air Act. Visiting parties of schoolchildren find much to amaze, and for many it is their first sight of an open fire. Having seen baking demonstrated, one seven-year-old girl wrote: 'The baker could tell if the fire was 'ot a nuff by putting his hand in the oven. When his hairs went brown he could tell.'

Netherton, $1\frac{1}{2}$ miles west of Dudley town, was created an ecclesiastical parish in 1844 when it was one of the largest in the country, but twenty-one years later it ceased to be so and became part of the borough of Dudley. It lies for the most part in a hollow so that the hillside church stands out sharply should one choose to descend from a point on the Rowley Hills close to a district called Springfield at Warrens Hall Park. Here about eighty acres of former pits and pit mounds have been converted into a conservation area, and the only surviving engine house of its kind in the Black Country, built in the 1820s and known as Cobb's, has been restored to represent the huge numbers that once littered the region. Not unlike Cornish engine houses familiar to holidaymakers, with structural variations obvious only to the expert, it is of brick construction with a ninety-five-foot-high chimney and was in operation until about 1928, becoming an empty shell when the James Watt engine was dismantled. However, an atmospheric winding engine housed in an adjacent building was purchased by Henry Ford, carefully demolished and crated and sent to a museum at Dearborn, Michigan.

Vandalism has undone some of the conservation work but this area is well worth visiting, not least because here is the Netherton end of the second and largest of the two tunnels to pass beneath the ridge, details of which have been given elsewhere. It was reopened in April 1984 after six years of closure to allow expensive repair work to be carried out, the timing being particularly fortunate with the legging tunnel temporarily closed to through traffic.

Warrens Hall Park, where no fewer than fourteen mine shafts were found and sealed, has natural and man-made pools stocked with fish and a stream coursing down – perhaps from the original spring of Springfield. As one walks into the dip beyond the engine house, several hump-backed canal bridges are to be seen, and beyond is the quaintly named Bumblehole, once a thriving boat-building centre. It is a simple matter to follow one's eyes through urban streets to the parish church of St Andrew's, Hill Street, with its broad avenue leading up through a churchyard lined with crumbling vaults and tombs. This is an imposing church, the bricks for which are understood to have been made locally and the stone quarried at Gornal. At 650 feet it has been declared the highest parish church in the country, a claim that could well be challenged but good enough for Black Country folk. It was constructed in 1830 as a chapel-of-ease to St Thomas' (Top Church) and restored and reopened in 1886 and again in 1913 when one of the pinnacles blew down in a gale and fell into the body of the church.

The oldest grave in the churchyard is said to be dated 1815, which suggests an earlier or temporary church, and those cholera victims of 1832 who were turned away from St Thomas' because its burial ground could take no more, are buried here in large unmarked common graves 'deeply dug' at the north-east side of the churchyard. Inside the church one is struck by the family box pews (listed) set in two rows between a wide aisle, and a large gallery on three sides supported on iron columns, indicative of the size of congregation anticipated. Of the many memorial tablets, the following, erected by parishioners, is unusual in text and although sadly undated reflects nineteenth-century poverty: 'A record of the gift of Mrs Blanche Skidmore to the church and parish. The east window, a peal of six bells, a bequest of £400 (consols) to provide a bible reader for the parish, a bequest of

£100 (consols) to provide warm clothes at Christmas for the poor communicants and a bequest of £100 to provide an annuity for the bell ringers.' Incidentally, this is one of the few churches I was able to enter without prior arrangement, then only because workmen chanced to be there, such is the dread of vandalism.

Proceeding down the hill from the church, Hill Street promptly changes to Highbridge Road and passes alongside Lodge Farm Reservoir, much utilized for water sport and as a general recreational area. Immediately beyond is the Saltwells Nature Reserve designated in 1981 and incorporating Blackbrook Valley and Saltwells Wood sloping down towards Pedmore Road with its accumulation of trading estate premises.

Close to this area and virtually a part of it is an unusual, one might think impossible, Black Country attribute – a healing saline spring, the Saltwells. Throughout its checkered history it has had various names, Lady Wood Spa being perhaps the best known by reason of a much reproduced advertisement of 1831 in which the mineral water is described as 'one of the best in the United Kingdom for almost every disease incident to the human body'. Grand claims were made for the cure of 'cutaneous eruptions without medical assistance' and that a man thus afflicted so that 'his body, head, hands and feet having assumed the appearance of leprosy ... by bathing and drinking the water was completely cured'. Bearing in mind that the year after it was written was that of the cholera epidemic, with health and hygiene considerations virtually nil, it is hardly surprising that many frightened people who could afford to do so clutched at this straw, but it did not come up to expectation either then or later and the project failed, only to be revived later in the century and to struggle on until the 1920s, being demolished a decade later. The industrial archaeology section of the Black Country Society carried out a survey of the former buildings and subsequently published its findings.

This same association played a major part in the restoration of the Mushroom Green Chainshop, not far from the Saltwells, plugging away at the authorities for three years in an attempt to prevent demolition of the nineteenth-century chainshop and attendant cottage. In the event the European Architectural Conservation Year (1975) tipped the scales in favour, the borough purchased the chainshop from its owners, and it was virtually rebuilt in the traditional style, preserving all that was possible. In 1976 it was handed over to the Black Country Museum, who fitted it out with chainmaking tools and equipment either donated or already in store. As a result this conservation effort by volunteers and the local authority enables parties of visitors to see chain made by hand in traditional surroundings just as it was in hundreds of Black Country chainshops until hand chain-making died out in the 1960s.

As we have seen at Warrens Hall Park, Netherton was an intensive mining area, and in 1808 the method of getting the thick coal and ventilating the mine workings, known as the Staffordshire Square Work Method, was first tried out there and eventually used in all Lord Dudley's collieries and in most of the thick coal seams of South Staffordshire. Ironworks and furnaces abounded, one of the most famed being that of Noah Hingley & Sons, who introduced ships' anchor manufacture to his works in 1848, installing two years later the first James Nasmyth steam-hammer to be used anywhere in the Black Country. Hingley's were to produce anchors, chain and chain cable for many of the giant ocean liners, including the anchor for the *Titanic*. A photograph exists of this anchor being taken out of the works on a flat wagon, and although they don't all show, it needed a team of twenty horses to haul it. According to men who worked at Hingley's at that time, the cable chain for this anchor was not the largest, having $3\frac{3}{8}$ inch-diameter links against some of four inches or more made entirely by hand, the steam-hammer being used to make six-inch-diameter links. One old hand recalled how in the early 1920s he had to go each morning to the Pack Horse public house by Netherton church and fetch beer in two buckets for the workmen. This would be what was termed 'near beer', a weak brew to quench the thirst of perspiring strikers as they swung the heavy sledgehammers to forge the white-hot metal into links.

Grazebrook's is another firm of historic importance, having been based at Netherton since the beginning of the nineteenth century as ironfounders, still in existence, but no longer a family concern. The fact that it is located in Pear Tree Lane should not be taken as indicative of an orchard setting since it is only one of a number of firms hereabouts. Here Grazebrook's received the blueprints to make the 8,000-pound bombs of World War II, the

first of which is said to have been dropped by a specially
equipped Lancaster on the Gnome works at Limoges in 1942.
This firm also possessed a James Watt engine of historic
importance, and this was eventually presented to the
Birmingham Science Museum, now installed at Dartmouth
Circus close to the Aston Expressway in Birmingham as a
monument to Watt's genius.

Industry at Netherton was certainly varied. Take on the one
hand Samuel Lewis (still existing), established in 1750, makers
of hand-formed nails, chains and harrows, and John Barnsley,
nowadays manufacturers of lifting gear but famous for a very
strange instrument – the jews (or jaws) harp, made in brass and
iron and described as a primitive musical instrument which,
when pressed against the teeth and twanged with the edge of the
palm of the hand, gave off tones of varying pitch by changes in
the velocity of the air intake. Vast quantities were made,
particularly between 1873 and 1880, and most were exported.
Horace Walpole is said to have grumbled that, in the American
colonies, 'Maryland was bought from the Indian with a quantity
of vermilion and a parcel of jaws harps.' Yet again, you name it,
someone in the Black Country made it!

There is little of note in Netherton streets beyond the normal
mishmash of urbanization except for the Old Swan public house
in Halesowen Road, no ordinary hostelry. Under the Pardoe
family it became known throughout the region and beyond, a
mecca for real-ale lovers. In the old days nearly everyone in the
Black Country brewed their own beer despite the large number of
pubs, and a working-class dwelling without a brewus (brew
house) was a rarity. A true home-brewed pub is one where the
beer is brewed and sold on the premises, and this is how it was at
the Old Swan when Ma Pardoe died in 1984. The pub's brew had
long been approved by the Campaign for Real Ale group, and
when it became known that the premises were for sale they
stepped in to prevent its being modernized by new owners,
subsequently floating a company to take it over.

Joseph Darby was a publican and his pub was the Albion in
Stone Street, Dudley, which he kept after retirement and is one
reason why he is frequently thought to be a Dudley man, whereas
he was born at Windmill End, Netherton, in 1861. Another
reason is that his collection of belts and trophies amassed for the

unusual sport of spring jumping is held in the museum in St James' Road, Dudley, to which they were presented after his death in 1937. They are well worth seeing but it is as well to enquire before visiting to make sure they are on display. Spring jumping is now unheard of in the way Darby practised it. His incredible feats are well authenticated and include the following out of a long list:

    ... Clearing half a dozen chairs with a jump taken off an ordinary glass tumbler filled with water, without spilling a drop.
    ... Achieving a backward spring jump of 12'11".
    ... Clearing a full size billiard table lengthwise minus the cushions, taking off from a block of wood.
    ... Making a double spring on to the surface of water and off again, wetting only the soles of his feet.

One of his earliest feats, done to astonish workmates in the days when he was a blacksmith, was to clear the canal in two jumps, making his second leap from the surface of the water. Perhaps it was this kind of exhibition that resulted in a career as a showman, and even after retirement he would entertain customers at the Albion by jumping on and off eggs without breaking them. Nor was his fame only local, for on 10 November 1888 Josey, as he was called, appeared at Evan's Supper Room, Covent Garden, London, in a 'command performance' before the Prince of Wales and other members of the royal family. By that time he was world champion, a title he held until 1898.

5

Wolverhampton and Bilston

Wolverhampton is a town in which it is necessary to tread warily when linking it with the Black Country. For this reason I shall ignore residential areas such as Tettenhall and Pendeford, which by no stretch of the imagination can be included. As to the rest, and here I refer to the old pre-Bilstonized Wolverhampton, there are historic pointers to warrant inclusion. One such is the borough coat of arms, which incorporates a brazier as 'being indicative of the Black Country', another is the fact that when in 1866 Queen Victoria visited the town to unveil an equestrian statue to the Prince Consort, a great triumphal archway of coal was erected near the railway station. Coal equates with Black Country, so why, if the town is not part of it, did the nineteenth-century dignitaries, conscientious and aglow with civic pride, regard an arch of coal as an ideal symbol with which to impress? One such excuse perhaps is that it was all they could think of at short notice, for the Queen's visit came only nine days following her acceptance of the invitation and must have put the authorities in a flap. In fact, Wolverhampton was the first town to be honoured with a visit since the death of Albert, and it was during this journey, as one is always being reminded – apocryphal though it might be – that she had the blinds drawn over the windows of her carriage as the train passed through the region from Birmingham so that her eyes should not be offended by the scenes of squalor and industrial detritus visible from the railway in this most wealth-producing centre of her realm.

Whatever the strength of such evidence, coal certainly was mined not far from the town centre, and townsfolk suffered from colliers betimes, such as during the riots of 1831, when the entire region was in uproar and Wolverhampton magistrates had to send to Birmingham and Stafford for military assistance. There is also on record the location of a coal forest near to the town centre at Parkfield, where in the space of one acre the stumps of seventy-three trees with their roots attached were found, the trunks lying prostrate in every direction and the roots forming part of a stratum of coal ten inches thick. We are told that below this was a second forest, and five feet below lay yet another: it must have been a remarkable geographical find, sadly not preserved.

But long before the need to wrest coal from the earth became paramount Wolverhampton was commercially prosperous as a wool-trading centre and was recognized as such by Parliament by the mid-fourteenth century. Wool was to predominate for nearly two hundred years, and one sixteenth-century family who had made fortunes in the trade built the Lea at Penn, once an estate, now commemorated in the name of a road. Carved over the doors of the houses owned by this family were the words 'I thanke my God and always shal. It was the sheepe that payed for al' [sic]. In the town, names such as Fold Street, Mitre Fold and Wadhams Fold exist as reminders of the trade.

Among the wealthy wool-merchants was Sir Stephen Jenys, founder of Wolverhampton Grammar School. The Mander Centre occupies part of the school site, and a plaque – one has to look above one's head to spot it – tells us that, 'In 1512 Sir Stephen Jenys, Lord Mayor of London, founded Wolverhampton Grammar School in buildings on this site. Between 1712-1717 they were reconstructed by the Merchant Taylors Company, the then trustees of the school, and served their original purpose until the year 1874, when the school was moved to Compton Road. After being put to various uses they were demolished in 1964 as part of the central town development scheme ... This tablet was erected by the Governors of Wolverhampton Grammar School.'

As will be seen, the town was to switch from wool to the metal trades, but first one should stay with the distant past and take a look at the fine sandstone church, no part of which is earlier than the thirteenth century, although, as already mentioned, it originated in Saxon times. Most of what is visible today including the tower is fifteenth-century although the chancel was completely rebuilt in the 1860s. It is an imposing structure standing slightly above the level of the town, its well-kept churchyard gardens fronting busy Lichfield Street. Originally the Catholic Church of St Mary, it became St Peter's in Henry III's reign, and it is a pity that it is closed to visitors, for a translation of Lady Wulfrun's charter of A.D. 994 is inside, as are monuments linking with the town's history including those to wool-merchants such as the Levesons, ancestors of the dukes of Sutherland (a branch of whom is said to have lived at a moated hall where the public library now stands), and the Lanes, renowned for having helped Charles II escape to Bristol following his meanderings to Boscobel and elsewhere after the battle of Worcester.

Fortunately the town's most ancient relic stands outside the church for all to see, seemingly to huddle as close as possible to the south porch as protection from vandals and surrounded by railings. It is a Saxon preaching cross confidently asserted to be mid-ninth century, not really a cross but a fourteen-foot-high circular pillar with a decorated shaft too weathered for clarity. Also in the churchyard gardens stands a bust mounted on a plinth, separated from the Saxon pillar by almost a thousand years. It is to one Douglas Morris Harris, AB RNVR and bears the inscription: 'This heroic wireless operator continued to record messages in the log on the shell torn drifter Floand until killed by enemy gun fire. Adriatic Sea. March 15, 1917.'

Close by is a fountain dated 1894 inscribed to Philip Horsman in recognition of his gift of the art gallery and other philanthropic deeds. Adjacent is the art gallery and museum itself, opened in 1895 and today a much-loved asset actively supported by a group of friends. A two-storey Italianate structure with sturdy columns, it is notable for a lack of windows to the upper floor, wisely providing a greater length of wall space for display purposes, daylight illumination being provided by skylights.

Queen Square, from which access to St Peter's can be gained via Lich Gate or Exchange Street, is the main town square – formerly High Green – where the equestrian statue of Prince Albert stands on a plinth which informs passers-by that it was erected by public subscription. Lich Gate has no gate but is a brick-built house dating to the early eighteenth century, whilst in Exchange Street there is a plaque to Dame Maggie Teyte, prima donna, born in Wolverhampton in 1888, although she is said to have despised the town. The tenth child of a wine-merchant and public house owner, she became one of the world's best-loved operatic artists but was a sad, near-bankrupt figure when she died at the age of eighty-eight.

Over the years Queen Square has seen considerable alteration to meet traffic needs and general redevelopment, a reminder of which is an entrance to the Mander Centre, the main shopping complex completed in 1970 with shops on two levels surrounding a precinct and incorporating the ten-storey Mander House and a multi-storey car-park that can really bring one's car within yards of the shops for those fortunate enough to find the best spaces. This Centre is superior to the Wulfrun Centre with which it is linked, the latter commemorating the town's ninth-century lady bountiful, and it is worth examining how the name Mander ties in with one of the town's basic metal trades, although today the name is synonymous with paint.

The founder of the Mander business, Benjamin Mander, was born in 1752 and lived in John Street where he tried to make a fortune as a japanner and tin-plate worker, then a growing local industry. His younger brother John had other ideas and in 1773 founded a chemical 'factory', being one of the first to make the various mercurial preparations then used extensively in medicine and the arts. He moved to what is now Victoria Street and subsequently bought land adjacent to that of Benjamin, already occupying between them a prime slice of the town. It was Benjamin's only son Charles who was to steer the Mander name towards the paint business when he began to show an interest in the mixtures of rosin, oil and turpentine, using the kitchen stove before being banished to the bottom of the garden, where he established his first varnish works. Actually he hadn't diversified from the family business entirely because varnish was complementary to his father's japan trade, being used by artists for decorative work. Indeed, when competition became particularly fierce in 1815, it was decided to bolster up the japan trade by making more varnish. Thus a lad's annoying kitchen experiments were to lay the foundations of a great twentieth-century firm. But it wasn't easy, as the following account of

Charle's efforts to sell varnish illustrate. Date, November 1817:

> I left Bristol at six o'clock and arrived at Bridgewater soon after twelve o'clock, where the only coach maker kept an inn, at which of course I dined. Before dinner I got an interview with the landlord with whom I had some difficulty to give my varnish a trial. He said he did all his business with Mr Ives and had done so for more than twenty years, except when he had been persuaded to try some other, of which he had always repented ... I soon got the ear of the son who took two quarts from me and promised he would give it an immediate trial himself, and if he approved of it, the next time I came he would give me an order ...

How revealing is that statement: so far for so little and he could not have carried many quarts per trip. A modern rep may well blanch, yet that is how many of today's giant enterprises came into being, and for sheer effort and perseverence as much as for product development the name Mander is rightly perpetuated in a shopping centre which in part occupies the site where Manders began to make varnish over two hundred years ago. Today the company's factory is at Heath Town, out in the suburbs.

When Benjamin Mander was born, Wolverhampton had a population of about eight thousand and was very much a market town with its corn exchange, weekly market and horsefair, occupying the area around the church and High Green, but with a vital nucleus of industry in the metal trades. The first big change in outward development was the building of a second church in the 1760s, said to bear a similarity to St Martins-in-the-Fields, London, and forming the centre of fashionable square now sliced into by a ring road and rows of parking meters. At that time the town finished at North Street, Piper's Row and as far as the new church on the Dudley Road just beyond Snow Hill, but following the appearance of canals in the early 1770s there was a spread outwards to make use of this improved method of transporting goods, so much easier than using the still very bad roads.

Among the new arrivals at the end of the eighteenth century was a man by the name of Bayliss, a blacksmith from Shropshire who started a smithy near Monmore Green on the Bilston side of the town. His son William, born in 1803, was just twenty-three years old when he founded, sufficiently close to the canal for an arm to be built, a firm that grew into one of the town's greatest, now alas no more. Yet when I started work there in 1934 it looked solidly entrenched on both sides of the road, seemingly to prosper for ever. One of its departments made wrought-iron gates, and I was just in time to see the last of the blacksmith-craftsmen who could shape iron as a child shapes plasticine. Uneducated in a conventional sense, they formed metal scrolls round chalkmarks drawn on the floor, and produced decorative features with open hearth, hand-bellows, anvil and hammer – sustained by tea you could stand a spoon in, brewed on the glowing fire.

Some men preferred cold tea. 'I cor get me tay bottle in me pocket, me wench,' shouted the departing workman to his wife upstairs. 'Then pour a drop out, yer fule,' she shouted down. Yes: an old joke that fails to do the Black Country man justice. He is not 'thick'. TV documentaries about the region tend to portray him as such, or as an uncouth drunkard or bigot. The rough, kindly humour such as I experienced seems to have got lost in time. In the days of Empire men such I have described made ornamental gates for the palaces of ruling princes, tall enough for elephants to pass through. Nearer home this particular firm also made the entrance gates to Stormont Parliament, Belfast, whilst much of their work was needlessly destroyed to 'help' the 1939-45 war effort.

The japan tin trade engaged in by Benjamin Mander had made its first tentative appearance as early as 1720, allegedly from South Wales, and improvements in design and manufacture created a new breed of skilled men of artistic ability. The process of japanning is the coating of sheet metal with a hard jet black lacquer, in imitation of Japanese lacquer. The skill lay in producing elaborate fine gold lines and decorative designs on fire screens, tea trays and other articles, and whilst the trade had its ups and downs it continued into the present century and is still recognized as superior work. The year 1850 was so prosperous that the National Trades Association of London sent delegates to the principal tin-plate manufacturers to inform them that the workmen in their employ were dissatisfied with their wages, especially as pay differed between firms. A proposal to standardize prices was accepted by two firms, whilst others hedged. Trouble flared when a firm called Perry did not give in to demands and dismissed a man for inciting resistance, drawing the full wrath of the Association. A strike began which lasted for eight months, during which no orders were fulfilled; then Perrys imported French tinmen, only to see them 'bought off' by the trade association and sent home. Undaunted, the company sent for German tinmen, and so that they should not be got at, it was arranged that they should work, live and sleep on the premises. This enraged the strikers, violence ensued and a number of men were indicted for conspiracy. Ultimately the men were sent to prison and the cost caused the Association to become bankrupt. It is said that Perry helped to pay outstanding costs and that from then on the manufacturers were left in peace for nearly thirty years. This dispute serves to underline the importance of the trade in Wolverhampton.

Although the lock trade is rightly credited to Willenhall, Wolverhampton had an early involvement. Thomas Gibbons – a company still flourishing as James Gibbons but in another trade – claims to be the oldest firm of lockmakers in Britain, founded in 1670, although little is on record before 1858, when a surviving document reveals a grievance of workers which was more localized than that of the tin-plate workers. It is in the form of a round robin signed by twenty lockmakers (no fools they) who had become dissatisfied with the clerk. According to them, he was 'scarcely ever sober and at times hardly able to settle our accounts as regards our reckoning at work ... We ask nothing but what is fair and just to put our work down and state what money we are going to receive in the morning and not have to have it altered at night for it makes things very unpleasant. We wish to have our work put down in ink and not like it is at present in black lead ...' To a Black Country person, black lead has always meant a pencil, although it is also a substance used by women to polish the fire grate and fittings to make them gleam. Such is the way of speech: they knowen what they mean! (Gibbons' went on to become a pioneer of the anodizing process in the 1920s and remained a private company until 1966.)

Another Wolverhampton metal industry is that of process finishing, for in 1839 galvanizing was introduced locally on a large scale, and it is said that for a time more galvanized iron was produced in the vicinity than anywhere in the world. But to return to lockmaking, Chubbs – basically a London firm – opened a factory in Wolverhampton in 1818, and still operate a plant there.

A year after galvanizing was added to the town's industries there came an important innovation in the manufacture of holloware when a patent was taken out for enamelled cast iron. Domestic holloware production flourished with the advent of steam-operated stamping machinery, and the new shapes won a gold medal at an exhibition in Melbourne in 1888 – more success for Wolverhampton. In that same decade two engineers, Thomas Parker and Bedford Elwell, began a venture which ultimately became the Electric Construction Company of modern times. These men provided what is believed to be the earliest instance of underground lighting in this country, at collieries in the Forest of Dean, and they went on to pioneer tramway construction.

It is hardly surprising that with so much industrial development the population soared from 12,500 in 1801 to nearly 50,000 in 1851 and almost 95,000 in 1901, and that working folk came off badly for accommodation and services. Various improvement acts from 1814 included the construction of Darlington Street, named after the Earl of Darlington from whom the land was purchased and which itself became a problem because at the backs of houses on one side ran an open sewer. Cholera struck in 1832 (193 deaths) and in 1849 (720 deaths), and in 1872 there were over 200 deaths from scarlet fever. An orphan asylum set up in 1849 to care for children who had lost both parents in the plague was destined to become the prestigious Royal Wolverhampton School.

Considerable study has been carried out on the state of housing in Wolverhampton during the eighteenth and nineteenth centuries, and it is not a pretty story. Not until the extensive council house building boom of the 1920s-30s was the problem really tackled, and I would think that the large Low Hill estate would seem comparable to the Priory estate at Dudley. Whilst the war interrupted slum clearance, the task was resumed in the 1950s, Wolverhampton claiming to be the first to submit a scheme when it became possible to do so.

Wolverhampton became a borough in 1848, its first mayor being George Benjamin Thorneycroft, which brings us to the more traditional ironworking aspect of Black Country industry. In 1924 he joined his brother Edward at the Shrubbery Ironworks in Walsall Street, nearer to the town centre than Monmore Green yet described then as a suburb. Here he proposed to 'turn iron stone into gold', and the coming of the railway age in the 1830s could hardly have been more fortuitous, for he grasped the requirements and became an authority on the manufacture of malleable iron and on railway wheels and axles. Unexpectedly, the works closed during a recession in 1877 whilst still in good shape. Criticized he may have been, but G.B. Thorneycroft remained a leading figure in the town, and when he died in 1851 an estimated twenty thousand people attended his funeral. A marble statue was placed in the vestibule of the old town hall, now law courts, when it was opened in 1871, and it is there still.

Whereas in earlier times the home had been the place of work, with a smithy or workshop attached, the growth of the factory system induced people to live as close to their employment as their legs could carry them. The well-to-do and managerial classes rode horseback or used coaches, but within two years of the Birmingham Canal being opened, 'express' flyboats began to operate between Birmingham and Wolverhampton. Pulled by two horses, changed every four to six miles and averaging speeds of eight to ten miles an hour, they had heated cabins and provided a smoother ride than any stagecoach. A verse of the 1780s ran:

For here a cabin in each end is found,
That doth with all convenience abound.
One at the head, for ladies nine or ten
Another at the stern for gentlemen.
With fires and tables to sit at ease,
They may regale themselves with what they please.

Flyboats had priority over other traffic, but whilst they may sound reasonable, it is difficult to imagine how they were able to pass dozens of laden narrow boats: there must have been much deft throwing of tow-lines and, although not advertised, much foul language from working boatmen. Nevertheless, a regular service was operated for around fifty years and together with the stagecoach provided the main means of communal travel until 1852, when the Oxford & Worcestershire Railway reached Wolverhampton, followed by the Shrewsbury-Birmingham and the Great Western, the latter taking over the other two in 1854. Five years later a new industry began to develop, that of locomotive-building, with over a thousand men employed in 1879. Hundreds of locomotives were built in Wolverhampton, and when the GWR broad gauge was abolished, it was debated whether Wolverhampton or Swindon should become the chief locomotive-building works. Swindon won, supposedly because land there was cheaper. However, locomotive works continued at Wolverhampton until 1964.

So now ordinary folk could travel where the railways spun their metal threads, and during the early railway mania the Black Country was criss-crossed by a network of ridiculous proportions. Even so, the machine that really brought cheap, go-where-you-please travel, ideally suited to the metal trades of Wolverhampton, was the bicycle. By the end of the 1860s the velocipede had arrived from France and seized public imagination, and among the first British models to achieve national acclaim were those built in Wolverhampton by Daniel Rudge, although when he died his business was moved to Coventry and only cycle historians and enthusiasts now link him with his home town. No fewer than fifty-nine Wolverhampton cycle manufacturers have been located as having existed in the 1890s against only nine elsewhere in the Black Country.

Henceforth the town was to play a part in all forms of transport development. John Marston, a successful japanware manufacturer, was urged to make bicycles, and in 1887 his first 'safety' was produced. This marked the start of the famous Sunbeam cycle which in 1907 was claimed to 'represent the highest quality and durability for finish ever introduced into the manufacture of a bicycle'. The Sunbeam company progressed under the Marston family to make motorcycles and cars, building up to earn an enormous reputation among a growing motoring public in sport, a milestone in motor-racing history occurring in 1923 when Henry Seagrave (knighted in 1929) won the French Grand Prix, a Sunbeam being the first British car to take this 'blue ribbon of motoring'. Later came the world land speed record bid when in 1927 a Sunbeam racing car, again with Seagrave at the wheel, made motoring history by being the first to exceed 200 m.p.h. – on the twenty-three mile Daytona Beach, Florida, USA.

Sunbeam engines were used on aircraft and airships, and by 1931 the company were making trolley buses which ran on Black

Country routes and were sold abroad in large numbers. This once great firm – Sunbeamland – now no more, is worthy of special tribute in any assessment of Wolverhampton. It is pinpointed today by the Sunbeam public house on the Penn Road and nearby Sunbeam Street and Marston Road. The area is now occupied by a miscellany of firms utilizing old factory premises.

However, Sunbeam were by no means the only producers of petrol-driven vehicles in Wolverhampton: AJS motorcycles made their appearance in 1897 and became frequent winners of the Isle of Man TT Races; Clyno Cars appeared in the early 1920s and by 1926 it was the third biggest motor-manufacturer in the country. Further out of town Guy Motors had come into being as early as 1914 and in addition to building lorries diversified in 1919 to make charabancs. By 1926 the company was exporting buses by the hundred, and also produced Britain's first six-wheeled double-decker trolley bus. In 1961 Jaguar Cars bought out Guys, so that has gone also.

This survey of Wolverhampton's diverse manufacturing base leads to the conclusion that the town pioneered a whole lot of high-flier industries which it somehow lost to Coventry, Birmingham and elsewhere, and one can only reflect on how much larger it would have been had it held on to them. Add the fact that it *might* have had Swindon's locomotive works and who knows what its present size might have become.

Perhaps because it is an industrial town, it does not have a very good record for preserving historic buildings. All the old coaching inns have gone, and the Deanery, described as perhaps the loveliest seventeenth-century building ever to have been erected in Wolverhampton, was demolished in 1921, its site now occupied by a College of Technology. Built on the site of a medieval dwelling, it is said to have had Wren characteristics.

The principal ancient building to survive, looking very much out of place wedged in among the Mander Centre complex at the corner of Victoria Street and St John's Street, is a sixteenth-century timber-framed building restored during 1979-81 and used as a welfare centre. In Darlington Street the chapel still survives with its large dome, impressive when it was built in 1900 and now scarcely noted, whilst at the bottom end of North Street, past the combined Civic and Wulfrun Halls which are housed under one roof and are a focal point of much of the town's social life, are Giffard House and church. The Giffards were an ancient Roman Catholic family linked by marriage to the Levesons and supporters of the King in the Civil War. Giffard House is remarkable because it is actually built into the church – or the church into the house! Once part of a fashionable area, this joint structure, dated 1728, stands alone and sadly out of place in a modern setting. A better-known reminder of the Giffard family is the Giffard Arms in Victoria Street. Retracing one's steps along North Street, one comes to the very modern and much criticized new Civic Centre.

A former building of distinction was the Old Hall, home of the Levesons, converted in the eighteenth century into a tin and japan works and demolished in 1883. The public library partly covers the site, but a walk round the back brings one to Old Hall Street to serve as a reminder. Here too is the Adult College covering subjects 'from art to yoga'. Wolverhampton is strong on educational facilities, and the College of Technology and College of Art and Craft are both senior colleges associated with the Polytechnic which was established in 1969 and has spread itself considerably.

Since education is based on an ability to read, it is worth mentioning that the town had its own newspaper as early as 1789 but somehow lost it in 1793, to be revived in 1811. It is a regrettable reflection on our times that this paper survived right through to 1980 when it was merged with a 'giveaway' and lost its distinction as the oldest newspaper in Staffordshire. However, a major evening paper has endured to celebrate its centenary in 1974 when the proprietors presented the town with a statue of Lady Wulfrun. Sculpted by the late Sir Charles Wheeler, a Freeman of Wolverhampton, it can be seen between the Civic Centre and St Peter's, surely one of the few statues to commemorate a tenth-century female. Nice thought!

The town has held firmly to its ancient market charter, the old market hall and market having been replaced by a modern market hall and adjacent open market-place in Salop Street. Recipient of a Civic Trust award, it was opened in 1960 and like all Black Country markets is highly regarded. As one walks around the town, it is apparent that the whole central area is designed to cater for shoppers, for in addition to the Mander and Wulfrun Centres large sections of former main streets – Dudley

Street and Queen Street in particular – are paved. A ring road has existed in a roughly western arc for well over a decade and in conjunction with redevelopment generally has fitted in fairly unobtrusively. The eastern part of the ring road has very nearly been completed. However, one must cross the ring road to reach what to most people throughout the UK and even abroad equates most with the name Wolverhampton, namely the Wolves Football Club, whose ground is at Molineaux. Once the home of an ironmonger named Benjamin Molineaux, the house and grounds have had a varied history. They remained in the family until the 1860s, and the grounds were laid out as terraced gardens, subsequently advertised as 'pleasure gardens' where such events as cycle-racing took place. The house eventually became a hotel, and in 1869 the South Staffordshire Industrial and Fine Art Exhibition was held there. The vandalized house, empty since 1979, is now a listed building whilst the grounds form a part of the famous football ground.

Wolverhampton Wanderers Football Club was founded in 1887 and moved to Molineaux two years later. The club was one of the original twelve members of the Football League and won the FA Cup in 1893 as well as three times in the present century, but the team is not as good as it used to be. I well remember in the 1930s hearing workmen say to one another, 'Did yer goo down Sat'day?' *Down* was always to the Wolves ground. Everyone discussed the team's performance, and when a mid-week cup-tie was played local works were so depleted of labour that they closed for the half day. And this was during a depression when loss of pay could be ill afforded, such was the power of the club.

Having ventured across the ring road, at the risk of putting a leg outside my designated Black Country, one should venture into the nearby West Park, opened in 1881 and covering some fifty acres, originally the site of a race course. Here stands the statue of Sir Charles Pelham Villiers, wretchedly smeared in multi-coloured graffiti but interesting in that he represents another renowned industrial family, for Villiers was famous for motorcycle engines. There is still an industrial engine factory bearing the Villiers name. Incidentally, close to Villiers' statue there is a giant block of Felsite supposed to have been carried during a glacial epoch from Merionethshire and found in the town in 1881. In 1902 the West Park was the scene of

Wolverhampton's attempt at an industrial exhibition to 'emulate the London Exhibition of 1851' with purpose-built halls and a royal opening during which the ducal visitors received a real Black Country welcome, 'but with none of the roughness with which people in other parts generally associate the Black Country'. *Clang*! Unhappily the event proved to be a financial disaster.

Returning from the park to re-cross the ring road, there is to be seen in Park Crescent a Ukrainian church, although there is nothing to say that it is. It serves as a reminder of Wolverhampton's immigrant population which also includes Polish as well as West Indian and Asian communities, and a number of Dutch who were stationed locally during the war. Specific organizations cater for their needs, and the town has a good record in integration, though not of course without problems.

Back in the town one finds, or rather smells, yet another old-established industry – brewing. Several brewers and maltsters amalgamated to form the Wolverhampton & Dudley Breweries Company in 1890; more have been added over the years, including Julia Hanson whom we met at Dudley, and today the Park Brewery is the home of one of the region's favourite brews. Their hostelries are well patronized for most Black Country folk like a drink, and if entertainment is provided along with it, so much the better. That is why variety theatres fared well until TV came along and they began to close. Wolverhampton's Hippodrome was pulled down in the late 1950s to be replaced by a store, and the town is left with the offerings of the Civic and Wulfrun halls and of the Grand Theatre at the station end of Lichfield Street. Opened in 1894, the Grand was successful and much loved, becoming the home of a repertory company for twenty-five years and host to some of the most famed personalities from Edwardian Ellen Terry to young Charlie Chaplin (as a callboy), right through to stars like Norman Wisdom. But this is no everyday story of theatre life, for it went into decline and closed in the early 1970s. For over three years the town was without a theatre, incredible for a town of its size, and following hard-fought campaigning the building was saved from developers, refurbished at a cost of a million pounds and opened anew in 1983 with high hopes and extensive publicity. But within a year it was on the skids, and despite managerial changes and reprieves its future hangs in the balance. It seems that whilst local people want the theatre they are not buying tickets in sufficient numbers. Some are afraid to go out at night, and the fact that there is no car-park immediately adjacent is detrimental.

Now, however, I shall edge out of Wolverhampton, passing the modern British Rail station and an ugly old building at the corner of Horseley Fields which looks nothing at all but is a railway building believed to be of 1849 vintage, the original purpose of which is uncertain, and out along Piper's Row onto the Bilston Road, which takes one over the Birmingham Canal to Monmore Green. Here are the Wolverhampton Speedway Stadium and East Park.

The first documentary mention of Bilston is in Lady Wulfrun's Charter of A.D. 994. It was a royal manor until Henry III's reign, when the King granted Crown lands to Walter de Bilston for, so it is thought, his services at the battle of Evesham, and part of the de Bilston shield was incorporated in the coat of arms when Bilston became a borough in 1933. The first municipal charter (1824) was for 'establishing and regulating a market and for erecting a market hall and market-place. Coal and ironstone are recorded as having been mined at Bilston in 1315, and an output of ten million tons was logged in 1864, giving an indication of the huge extent of mining operations. Nevertheless, Bilston's fame has been associated with volume iron-production since John Wilkinson came to Bradley in 1757, right through the steelmaking era to the collapse of heavy industry in the region in the 1970s and '80s. When Boulton and Watt set up their foundry beside the Birmingham Canal at Smethwick, Wilkinson, was one of the first to appreciate Watt's improvements to the Newcomen engine. The two men were to be of immense benefit to each other, and without Wilkinson's support Watt's innovation would have been less successful, for Wilkinson devised a machine capable of boring Watt's cylinders to an accuracy not previously achieved so that he was able to boast an ability to 'provide customers with a 72-inch cylinder which could not be further from absolute truth than the thickness of a thin sixpence in the worst part'.

Actually, the boring of engine cylinders was what one would now describe as a spin-off, for Wilkinson was boring cast-iron

cannon with outstanding success: not only were they used in the
American War of Independence but it is said that during the
riots of 1790, when a mob threatened to attack the
Bradley works, he loaded up several twenty-four pounders of his
own manufacture and brought them into position in front of his
gates, whereupon the mob sensibly dispersed. Certainly he was a
man of great character, living and dreaming iron, seeing it as a
viable material for chairs, pulpits and coffins. He had his own
cast-iron coffin held in readiness, but when he died in 1808 it
proved too small and another had to be provided.

Like many ironmasters he issued trade tokens, halfpenny ones
showing a tilt-hammer motif on one side and a likeness of
himself on the other. This apparently bore a resemblance to
George III and prompted the *London Magazine* to print in 1787
the following:

So Wilkinson, from this example
Gives himself a matchless sample!
And bids the iron monarch pass
Like his own metal wrapt in brass!
Which shows his modesty and sense,
And how, and where, he made his pence.
As iron when 'tis brought in taction,
Collects the copper by attraction,
So, thus, in him 'twas very proper,
To stamp his brazen face on copper.

True to form, Wilkinson claimed never to write a letter
without the word 'iron' appearing in it. During his career he
engaged in all kinds of enterprises, not being averse to what in
those days were long and difficult journeys, such as going to Paris
in 1785 to help install forty miles of iron waterpipe for Paris
sewers. As was seen with Mander, eighteenth-century businessmen were prepared to win business on an eyeball-to-eyeball
basis. After his death the business was carried on by trustees, but
legal wrangling among his heirs and the slump which followed
the end of the Napoleonic Wars brought the Bradley works to
disaster, and they were sold in the 1830s. All that remains today
as a reminder of this remarkable man is a small monument in
Great Bridge Road, the plaque to which – cast in 1956 and now
vanished – was intended to tell the world that, 'Near this spot

John Wilkinson (1728-1808) erected his first blast furnace in 1757-8. It marked the beginning of the iron age in the Black Country and was truly the mother furnace of the district.'

With an abundance of minerals readily obtainable on the spot, ironworks proliferated and during the nineteenth century famous ironmasters such as Baldwin, Ward, Sparrows, Thorneycroft and Hickman were key figures. Baldwin's was one of the works belonging to the family that produced Worcestershire-born Prime Minister Stanley Baldwin, but it is the name Hickman that has to be carried forward to the historic Bilston Steelworks of blessed memory. 'Bilston illuminations' was how one described Hickman's steelworks in the 1930s, viewed across then derelict land from the Wolverhampton-Dudley Road between Sedgley Beacon and the Fighting Cocks public house. Iron had been made on this site, at the other side of Bilston to Bradley, since the 1780s. Acquired by Hickman's in 1866, it had five blast furnaces in operation by 1880 and continued to grow, being merged in 1920 with Stewart's and Lloyd's. Production continued until its last great phase in 1954 when the famous furnace *Elisabeth*, replacing three others, was lit and christened according to custom with the name of a female. Thus it became *Elisabeth* after the daughter of the company chairman and not 'Elizabeth' after the Queen! Following nationalization, the enterprise became the Bilston Steel Works, but by the early 1970s *Elisabeth* was the sole remaining blast furnace in the Black Country, a monument on the skyline to all that had gone before. Production ceased in 1979, and some two thousand men lost their jobs. When in 1980 the furnace was toppled into the dust, it marked the end of about two hundred years of blast-furnace ironmaking.

Bilston's other claim to fame, also some two hundred years old, is for enamelling. Eighteenth-century enamellers called themselves toymakers but their toys were not for children but for people of wealth and fashion. This fine-art craft, so ill-suited one would think to dingy backstreet workshops in the midst of collieries and ironworks, developed in Bilston in about 1750, probably even earlier but retarded by the Industrial Revolution which for a time would have overwhelmed and diverted interest from it. What were mere trinkets against the might of iron? But the enamellers prevailed in their objective of providing 'society' with such items as patch-boxes, snuff- and sweetmeat-boxes, scent-boxes, bonbonnieres and like items which followed the fashion of Versailles yet were considerably cheaper, being of copper rather than of gold or silver.

Bilston's location on the London-Holyhead Road would have helped, keeping the enamellers in touch with London. Considerable numbers of snuff-boxes were produced to commemorate the wedding of George III to Queen Charlotte in 1761. On the lid was a picture of the bride, inside that of the groom, and the box was inscribed:

Let him love now
Who never lov'd before.
Let him who ever lov'd
Now love the more.

Queen Charlotte made snuff-taking fashionable in feminine circles, many women using a small spoon to protect their nails. Apparently Bilston-made boxes were not to be sneezed at!

Bilston enamels require specialist study to identify, sometimes being confused with those made at Battersea, regardless of the fact that the latter factory was in existence for only some three years, from 1753, whereas the Bilston trade lasted for more than eighty years. The museum and art gallery at Mount Pleasant, Bilston, has a splendid collection of locally made enamels together with japanned ware and pottery. There is also a collection at Bantock House, located in a park a mile outside Wolverhampton town centre to the west. A patch-box on show there is inscribed: 'A trifle from Bilston' over a transfer of a large house, and bearing the name of one Sam Proud, described in the 1770s as a keeper of lunatics. Pottery, not generally associated with Bilston, was made originally of local clay, and exhibits in Bilston museum date from the 1870s, whilst japanning had been carried out in the area since 1719, before either Wolverhampton or Birmingham, so it is claimed.

Thus one finds these skilled trades co-existing with and subsequently making way for the heavy industries. It is perhaps ironic that, now the latter have virtually disappeared, enamels are again being made in Bilston by one enterprising company. Nevertheless, for all the industrial decline, Bilston is still home to world-famous companies that do not need to belch forth flame and smoke. Take one William Thompson who in 1834 began hammering rivets into plate to make boilers and founded a firm destined to produce some of the world's giant boilers and is now part of an international organization. Consider Joseph Sankey, born in 1826, who began his career making japanned tea trays. His firm went on to make holloware and over the next hundred years extended into the electrical and motor-body trades, existing today as GKN Sankey.

Unlike its enamels, Bilston is not a thing of beauty. It had many fine building but only one of note survives and that is the fifteenth-century Greyhound and Punchbowl inn, High Street, marred by being among shops. Generally thought (but disputed) to be the former manor house of Stow Heath, largest of the three manors of Wolverhampton, it became an inn some time during the eighteenth century but fell into a bad state of decay and might well have been demolished but for the help of a local brewery. Now restored, it is said by experts to look much as it would have five hundred years ago.

The town hall and parish church of St Leonard with its small churchyard form a block at the town's central road junction. The church is on a medieval foundation, the present building dating to 1826 and having a turreted tower and large gilt weathervane. The town hall was built in 1827 and originally housed a library. It is a very solid-looking structure with a clocktower, but built upon old pit workings so that by 1906 it was in such danger of collapse that it had to be shored up while the foundations were made safe. One of the town's most worthy characters, John Freeman (1853-1944) placed on record that mining was carried on in the centre of the town, 'the main streets thoroughly undermined by coal hunters'.

John Freeman was the town's humorist and chronicler of Bilston's oddities and eccentrics of the last century, writing of Edward Woolley, a noted manufacturer of screws, nicknamed 'Screw Oolley', of the Roaring Ratner who preached hell-fire and damnation, the bums (bailiffs) of whom the poor lived in dread, and the quack doctors with their cure-alls. At the back of the town hall is a plaque to the memory of another Bilstonian, John Etheridge (1772-1856), who 'sacrificed self and substance to the poor of this town'. Described by Freeman as Bilston's noblest son, Etheridge represents those practical aspects of philanthropy so necessary in his day, 'spending his Sunday for half a century in teaching miners to read the scriptures ... his humble shop the gratuitous depot for the sale of bibles and religious works a generation before reduced prices made them accessible through other means'.

Etheridge was fearlessly active through the cholera epidemics of 1832 and 1849, when among those who came to help in 1849 was Cardinal Newman in the role of assistant priest. As previously mentioned, Bilston was blamed for the outbreak in the Black Country, and nineteenth-century historian G.T. Lawley wrote that sanitation conditions were deplorable:

> Foulness and filth were seen in the old-fashioned streets; in the low courts and everywhere. Stagnant pools send up their deadly vapours, sink-holes their effluvia, and wretched hovels their thrice-breathed atmosphere. Undoubtedly the chief cause of this state of things arose from the character of the people who, brought together in great numbers by the demand for labour in the vast mines and forges of the town, were composed of the worst characters, morally and socially, that could possibly be conceived ... Being of degrading habits, and the houses numerically inadequate for the rapid influx of people, they herded together like swine, the filth of their tenements and their persons thus giving impetus to the blows of the avenger.

Such conditions prevailed throughout much of the Black Country but Lawley's character-assassination of Bilston people is harsh compared with the more humanitarian attitude of Freeman and Etheridge.

That section of Bilston's main thoroughfare known as Oxford Street is undergoing redevelopment, but the Church of St Mary the Virgin has been renovated following its 150th anniversary in 1980. Built when the population had become too large for St Leonard's, it has had a hard time: the porous stone used absorbed dust and grime, and it was damaged by fire in 1855 and sustained gale damage in 1925. However, this church is of particular interest because in its vicarage (now demolished) was born Henry John Newbolt (1862-1938), the celebrated poet who was to practise at the Bar from 1887 to 1899 and receive a knighthood. His published verses tended towards a naval theme, and why a man born just about as far from the sea as is possible in this tiny island should choose it as a subject is doubtless because his father, the Reverend Francis Newbolt, was the son of a captain in the Royal Navy. But a fine job Newbolt made of his writing, for how many generations of school children have recited 'Drake he's in his hammock an' a thousand miles away' from 'Drake's Drum', as well as those so-English public-school play-the-game lines: 'There's a breathless hush in the close tonight/Ten to make and the match to win' – so far in essence from his native Black Country.

Despite his mother having whisked him away to nearby Walsall at the age of four, when his father died, Bilston was loath to let Newbolt forget his birthplace and in 1927 he received at his Devon home a letter from the then Vicar of St Mary's, informing him that, to mark the centenary of the foundation of the church, the council was placing a tablet on the vicarage to record his birth, and that it was hoped he would come and unveil it. The poet was not overjoyed but came none the less, slept in the room that had once been his nursery, and toured the district. Contrasting the region of his boyhood with that of the late 1920s, he said that the Black Country was still to a certain extent a wilderness of man's own making.

Although the heavy industries have mostly vanished to create a new wilderness, Bilston remains a busy place, having its fair share of the industrial estates of small, single-storey units that have mushroomed throughout the region, particularly since the coming of the motorway network which attracted all sorts of businesses, mostly linked to service industries, because of ease of access to the country as a whole. One such bears the name Beldray, which I was not astute enough to realize without enlightenment is an anagram of Bradley, where industrialization began in earnest. Ah well! One doesn't *expect* that sort of thing at Bilston!

Apart from the Roman Catholic Church of the Holy Trinity, also in Oxford Street, there is little else of note, although Bilston market is a magnet for bargain-hunters for miles around, and the shopping centre is modern, with good parking facilities.

So now let us follow young Newbolt down the road to Walsall.

6

Walsall

Walsall is not at all put out by the fact that it does not rate a mention in Domesday. Perhaps the commissioners' horses were pointing in the wrong direction or it was misty on that particular day around the tiny settlement. Anyway the modern borough has acquired two Domesday settlements, and what's a hundred years or so when it possesses a charter believed to date from the early thirteenth century? It measures only 245mm × 280mm and is written in Latin, being a grant of rights by William Ruffuss ('The Red'), Lord of the Manor of Walessal, to the burgesses. This charter is prized as the earliest evidence of the town being a borough and therefore considerably more ancient than big brother Brum (Birmingham) eight miles distant.

Apparently Henry II had given Walsall to the Ruffuss family in or about 1159, and the Ruffusses (or Coppernobs, as redheads were called in the Black Country of my boyhood) were to hold the manor for some two hundred years. In 1390 it passed to the earls of Warwick, who continued to be lords of the manor until 1488, which is why the bear and ragged staff appear on the town's coat of arms. Normally associated with Warwickshire, the device comes as rather a surprise in a Staffordshire town, but of course the two counties adjoined virtually since the founding of the shires in the eleventh century until they became lost in the boundary reshuffles of modern times.

The town developed on the steep slopes of a limestone hill over five hundred feet high, on the top of which stands the parish church, probably replacing a Saxon church. Originally the Church of All Saints, now St Matthew's, it was built in the thirteenth century, altered in the fifteenth century and in 1819-22 rebuilt on the old foundations, only the tower, spire and chancel along with the thirteenth-century crypt being retained. We are told that the walls were so strong that gunpowder had to be used to blast them asunder. The tower clock replaced four sundials late in the eighteenth century, and the spire we see today is as recent as 1950.

Walsall has kept its documents well, for the list of incumbents, whilst incomplete, dates to 1211 and the registers to 1570. Also the list of mayors starts at 1377, and although the next entry jumps to 1452, it is the longest list in the traditional county of Stafford. Unhappily it is not possible nowadays to walk into the church, although the potential vandalism at St Matthew's can hardly compare with that sustained during the Civil War when the Roundheads used it as a barracks. However, closure does deprive the visitor of admiration of the fine stained glass windows of the chancel and the rood and screen in the nave, carved by skilled workers and erected in 1913. But one can admire and walk through an unusual vaulted archway located directly beneath the high altar, once part of a roadway.

Approaching the church from the High Street up about sixty steps, one is immediately in an area of tranquillity at odds with the bustle of the town below. The views here are extensive, and there is a seat at which to admire it and regain one's breath beside the tiny churchyard. There is a splendid lychgate to be examined, given in 1927 in memory of George and Catherine Gill, by their daughter, and restored in 1973 in memory of Alice Lucy Hope. Close by is the enclosed Church Hill war memorial garden with railed viewing areas for surveying the urban landscape. The first stone for this amenity was laid by Princess Margaret on 1 May 1951, and next to the garden is St Matthew's Close, a block of neat, low-rise flats whose tenants, looking out at the church and landscaped surrounds, must surely think themselves privileged: raised as they are above the town, they could well imagine themselves in some rural retreat. I found the whole Church Hill complex a gratifying 'find', not having previously ventured to climb those steps. Not to deceive: it should be added that of course there is a roadway at the back of the hill so no one need feel unable to get there.

What has been done here is particularly gratifying when looking at old illustrations and discovering that in bygone days the town clung to the hillside itself, roof surmounting roof, and that slums existed on the hill until the 1930s. From medieval until comparatively modern times the town encompassed only a small area extending down the hill and associated with the 'Foreign', a large area covering Bloxwich, Walsall Wood and Pleck, the latter name meaning waste. I read that 'Foreign' is an old manorial word, but to me it suggests that long before the Black Country was born locals tended to regard anyone living outside the immediate locality as being 'from off' – foreigners in fact!

In 1627 the town was favoured by Charles I with a municipal charter, and this was the term of reference for local government until the Municipal Corporation Act of 1835 reformed existing corporations everywhere. It marked the beginning of popular government and established the principle that councillors were individually responsible to ratepayers, abolishing the privilege of freemen, a class of men who by accident of birth were invested with the government of a town. In this Walsall was merely following orders, so to speak, but it was quick to implement and was the first town to have a professional police force under the Act. It consisted of one superintendent and three constables. No other Black Country town boasted a police force until 1839, when the county of Worcester adopted the County Police Act passed in that year, and even then Dudley was not included until 1845.

Walsall quickly followed other trends. It was the third town in the country to adopt the Free Libraries Act of 1857, which it did two years later within a building in Goodall Street, and it was one of the first towns to establish a cottage hospital (1863), so influential townsfolk were clearly alive to events outside as befitted a town whose basic industries were built on communication via horsepower. On the other hand, through no fault of its own Walsall did not have a link with the canal system until the early 1790s, whereas neighbouring Wednesbury had been 'canalized' since 1769, and when in 1837 the railway came over the horizon, it was $1\frac{3}{4}$ miles away at Bescot, a one-horse omnibus providing the final link with the town, as it was to do for a decade.

High Street, the main street of the medieval town leading
down from the church, forms part of what is now an extensive
paved area which extends along Digbeth and Park Street and
includes the Bridge. In fact pedestrianization accounts for a
major part of the town centre, and on Tuesdays and Saturdays
market stalls extend from the Bridge almost to the church steps
where once stood a market cross. This is a large and lively
market, overflowing into side streets, and because it is so strung
out it gives an impression of being bigger than those of other
Black Country towns. A map of 1824 shows a pig market in a
prime position off the High Street, and it was at that time
reckoned to be one of the largest of its type in the land. This
reflects the professional side of pig-trading but working men all
over the Black Country habitually kept a pig in the backyard
(some would claim in the house) until after the 1939-45 war. The
pigs would be taken to be killed at the slaughterhouse and the
bacon and ham salted and hung in the kitchen to await
consumption. The practice was the source of many a joke that
has passed into tradition.

''Is yer father in?'

'No 'e's in the pigsty. Yo'll see which 'is 'im ... 'e's got 'is 'at
on.'

A minister comes across an old miner looking at a Bible. 'Glad
to see you are reforming,' he remarked.

'It ay that,' was the reply. 'I'm lookin' for names ter gie me
pigs.'

That map of 1824 shows a large number of central areas
marked as gardens, so Walsall seems to have been a better place
in which to live than the core of the region, as evidenced by
Thomas Carlyle when, in that same year, he wrote that the whole
region burned like a volcano smelting fire. Yet one should not
suppose that ironworks were far away, for eleven years earlier a
Walsall historian had written of local iron furnaces which had
'converted the inestimable bowels of the earth into a source of
employment for thousands of ingenious artists'. It was the slum
dwellings of these 'ingenious artists' and their families which
despite the more open aspects of the town resulted in the spread
of cholera in 1832, when eighty-five people died out of a
population of some fifteen thousand, escaping relatively lightly
in comparison with Bilston.

Walsall stands on the eastern edge of the Black Country, limestone, ironstone and coal having been mined or quarried since the fourteenth century, open-cast mining being considerable between the sixteenth and eighteenth centuries. Limestone extraction has left problems, as will be seen later, but minerals apart the town is noted as a specialist centre for saddler's ironmongery, a trade which began in the sixteenth century. Those engaged in it are called 'loriners', and huge quantities of buckles, spurs, stirrups, bits and other implements for the horse were produced to win world markets. The antiquary Leland, visiting in about 1540, wrote: 'Waulleshall, a little town in Staffordshir ... ther be many smiths and bytte makers yn the towne. It longith now to the king and there is a parke of that name scant half a mile from the towne. At Waulleshall be pittes of se cole, pyttes of lyme ...' Incidentally, present day Park Street is named after Walsall Park which extended to Bentley and covered much of the Pleck. Once a royal park, it was split up in the seventeenth century.

But to return to the loriners, the buckle trade was so extensive that in 1792, when it was threatened by a new idea in footwear, a deputation sought the help of the Prince of Wales, 'fearing that if the stagnation caused by the patronage of shoestrings and slippers were continued, miseries, emigrations and other harsh consequences must surely ensure'. It is said that the Prince ordered that the new-fangled strings should be given up and buckle-manufacture supported, but by 1820 buckles had lost out. However, by that time the town had added leathermaking to its list of trades, and this had grown rapidly, having material ready to hand in the form of oak bark from nearby forests, hides from cattle and sheep in Shropshire and Warwickshire, and saddler's ironmongery at hand to provide the metal parts. It was indeed a natural progression, and all processes were carried out in the town, from tanning and currying through to finished articles. Today, whilst it is still noted for leather, manufacturers buy prepared hides from elsewhere, and it is doubtful if more than three per cent of the workforce is engaged in the trade, metal goods of various kinds predominating. An idea of the magnitude of the saddler's ironmongery trade during the nineteenth century can be gleaned from the fact that it produced more harness furniture than any other town in the world, covering anything from a set of solid silver furniture for an Indian prince to run-of-the-mill ornaments, rosettes and the engraving and chasing of heraldic coats of arms, monograms and crests for the nobility. There was also an involvement in horseshoe and nailmaking, although these products were more extensively produced elsewhere in the region.

One outstanding yet today little-thought-of aspect of the horse-equipment trade was that of whipmaking. Until steam-powered transport took over from the horse, the demand for all equine trappings was enormous. There were over a thousand varieties of whips and thongs using thread and cane, gut and whalebone, holly and thorn, and later a combination of steel and cane covered with gut or thread. One manufacturer described himself boldly as 'The Whipper of the World ... the only steam whip factory in the kingdom ... the largest plant ... the biggest output ... the newest designs.' No false modesty: no advertising agency, just hard, confident sell! Nor was it simply the variety of whips but the willingness and skills to personalize them, for in a catalogue dated around 1880 it was stated that: 'Arms, crests, mottoes or monograms can be embossed upon the mounts of the whips on receipt of a model or drawing showing what is required.' Think of all those Walsall-made whips still lying in hallstands, outbuildings and attics all over the globe!

Consider also the variety of saddles, ranging from the delicately embroidered job for long journeys in South America to the plain, workmanlike saddle for the English hunter, the tiny race saddle weighing perhaps a pound to the large patterns favoured by South African farmers, the light horse harness for American sulkies to the heaviest styles for cart, plough and dray. All were in the day's work. It is easy to enthuse about these Walsall trades, so worthy of somewhat detailed reminder here, being so different from the industries of the Black Country as a whole. Nor are they all obsolete, for an upsurge in leisure riding has brought a limited revival.

The Bridge is the centre of Walsall town but it does not have the appearance of a bridge. There are no parapets from which to look down upon flowing water, and the tall buildings on it must not conjure visions of a kind of Ponte Vecchio. It is in fact a large square, the brook somewhere beneath having been covered over since the 1850s so that it is difficult to imagine that this small waterway once separated the High Street from Park Street, and that although a footbridge had existed since the fourteenth century people would pay a penny during times of flood to be carried across on a pony!

The centrepiece of the Bridge is the statue of a woman, and when the original was unveiled in 1886 it had the distinction of being the first statue in England to be erected in memory of an uncrowned lady. This was the town's heroine, Sister Dora. Real name Dorothy Wyndlow Pattison, she was born in 1832, youngest daughter of the rector of Hauxwell near Richmond, Yorkshire. She was thirty-two years old when she entered the Christ Church Sisterhood, an Anglican convent, and adopted the name Sister Dora. In 1865 she arrived at Walsall cottage hospital to replace a sick colleague, and although after two months she went away, she was back by November, drawn perhaps by destiny for she was to stay for life.

Her courage, devotion to duty and nursing abilities are legendary in Walsall, the main incidents of her career summed up on four illustrative panels set into the pedestal above which her effigy stands, representing her in nurse's dress in the act of unrolling a bandage. One panel illustrates her self-possession and ability to direct under trying circumstances during an explosion at an ironworks on 15 October 1875 whereby eleven men were so severely burned that only two survived. All were nursed by Sister Dora, who scarcely left them day or night.

Another panel illustrates her love for the 'tender little ones' and shows her nursing a child on one knee and rocking another in a cradle while conversing with the children of the hospital. By her side are two convalescing patients, a boy and girl. The next panel represents a scene in one of the adult wards of the hospital in which she and a doctor are attending a patient, and is illustrative of her care and solicitude for the suffering. The fourth panel illustrates her sympathy with the bereaved and represents a 'dreadful colliery disaster that occurred on 14 November 1872 … Twenty-two men were entombed and all perished before they could be rescued, and during the time that the women waited at the pithead Sister Dora stayed with them.'

When the cottage hospital was opened, a system of voluntary nursing was virtually unknown, the only nurses heard of being those who had gone to the Crimea with Florence Nightingale, so that Walsall folk found the dress of a sister strange and the very name 'sister' so odd that at first there were doubts and suspicions that nurses were Romanists in disguise. During a second visitation of smallpox in one year (1875), when it was feared that the sickness would be as bad as before, Sister Dora volunteered to go to the isolation hospital herself so that people would have confidence in her and in sending sick relatives.

Her work for Walsall people was so much appreciated that in 1873 she was presented by railway workmen with a pony and carriage, a very upmarket equipage for one in her position. No stuffy matron, it transpired years later that she had had a secret love affair with an ironmaster from Dudley, and when she developed cancer, she kept that secret also – even from her doctor – so that in November 1878 her great hope of opening a new hospital was denied to her. She died on Christmas Eve of that year. Given her track record, it is not surprising that the townspeople should want a statue to her memory. What is surprising, considering how the passage of time diminishes public feeling toward celebrities, is that as recently as 1957, when the white marble statue had become badly affected by pollution, it was thought worthwhile to replace it with a bronze replica. Many people probably think the statue they see today is the original, but in the council house stands the plaster-cast model, the mould from which the replica was made. Quite lifesize it is too when not on a pedestal! So thanks to a great deal of goodwill almost eighty years after her death, Sister Dora still stands on the Bridge, exuding calm despite being adopted by pigeons. It is interesting to ponder on the immense changes that have taken place since she was first installed there, the most drastic being behind her so that she was spared, for example, the demolition of the George Hotel in 1933.

For over 150 years the George was the main hotel and chief coaching inn during the stagecoach era when at various times upward of a dozen coaches ran through the town. Long before Sister Dora knew it, the frontage had been renovated and a colonnade added, making it a distinctive architectural feature. In its place rose a hotel, said to be the most modern in the Midlands, but it didn't last long, and in 1979 it too was demolished and replaced by a shopping development.

There are seats for the weary for Sister Dora to gaze down on, but the once great feature of the Bridge, an ornate clocktower presented to the town in 1855, has gone, replaced by one of somewhat gaudy appearance. One piece of Victoriana to have survived is the nearby shopping arcade with arched roofs of iron and glass. Inside is an echo of a bygone world, yet the arcade seems to blend externally with such modern redevelopment as the 1980s Saddlers Centre, so it is easy to pass from one to the other without blinking – how conditioned one is to changes of pace and atmosphere! The Saddlers Centre gives access to the railway station, but whereas once the town was an important railway centre, it is now merely a terminal station connecting with Birmingham. Demolition of the former station created a great furore, the booking hall being described by that over-worked word 'unique'. Under pressure from conservationists the portico was carefully dismantled and placed in store for possible re-erection elsewhere.

Now let us pass through the Saddlers Centre into Bradford Street, noting the solid-looking nineteenth-century school of art and crossing the road to a house on the corner of Caldmore Road. This is Belsize House, birthplace of Jerome K. Jerome, described as Walsall's most distinguished literary figure, which seems rather an exaggeration since the Jerome family moved to Stourbridge when he was two years old, and thence out of the region to London. Slender though the claim is Walsall makes much of Jerome Klapka Jerome (1859-1927) whose best-selling novel *Three Men in a Boat* owes nothing to the Midlands, nor does his best-known play *The Passing of the Third Floor Back*, a morality play set in a boarding house. Nevertheless Jerome was honoured with the Freedom of the Borough on 17 February 1927, when he unveiled a plaque at his birthplace and was presented with a scroll and casket. An extant photograph of the author and his wife listening to a speech by the then mayor causes one to reflect as to what he might have been thinking, considering he had been back to the town only once before, to collect material for his autobiography. He died the following June, and his birthplace was named Belsize House after his last home in Belsize Park, London.

Walsall's claim to Jerome was strengthened in 1984 with the opening of a museum at the house, one room containing documents and general memorabilia, another being a period-piece reconstruction of a mid nineteenth-century parlour typical

The Manor House, a restored medieval building used as licensed premises, West Bromwich

Clock tower at Carters Green, West Bromwich. It was erected as a
memorial to Alderman Farley, five times mayor

Galton Bridge, Smethwick, largest canal bridge in the world when built in the 1820s. Immediately behind is John Smeaton's Summit Bridge of 1790.

Telford's deep canal cutting at Smethwick with electrified railway running alongside

PIT BANK WENCHES,
WEDNESBURY.

Pit bank wenches, Wednesbury *c.*1900

eft: St Bartholomew's Church on the landscaped Church Hill at Wednesbury

Right: This stone lock sculpture bears a wealth of information. It stands on a forecourt in Willenhall

The Bull Stake, Darlaston

Clock tower, Willenhall

The new public library, Stourbridge opened in
1985 retains the façade of the former market
hall. The town clock was made locally and dates
to 1857

Top of flight of Nine Locks
(but only eight) at the
Delph, Brierley Hill

of the kind he would have lived in. For good measure the Jerome family has given the author's desk to Walsall, but rather than being in the museum one is told that it is in the mayor's parlour at the town hall.

One cannot do better than follow it there, or nearly so, for the town hall is in Leicester Street, just round the corner and linked to the council house in Lichfield Street, where one can read an inscription on a stone to the affect that it was laid by HRH Prince Christian of Schleswig-Holstein in May 1902. Lichfield Street, at its town end, is an imposing tree-lined thoroughfare accommodating the civic/cultural core of Walsall. Here are the central library and art gallery which incorporate a splendidly informative local history department containing a large variety of saddler's ironmongery, leather goods and specimens of yet another local skill, brush-making, carried on since the 1760s and covering every kind of brush imaginable. Bristles were obtained from Siberia, Poland and India, with fibres from South Africa and Mexico, weeds from Italy and horsehair from America, Australia and China; ivory and bone, as well as wood, were used for brush backs and handles: it really is awesome to consider the world-wide ramifications of what might be thought of as a relatively minor industry.

Outside the central library is a statue to a native of Walsall, John Henry Carless, who was posthumously awarded the Victoria Cross 'for most conspicuous bravery and devotion to duty' on 17 November 1917 at the battle of Heligoland Bight. It was unveiled in 1920 by Rear-Admiral Sir Walter Cowan, on whose flagship, HMS *Caledon*, John Carless had served, and consists of a portrait bust cast in bronze by a Wolverhampton man, R.J. Emerson, set on a base of Portland stone. Provided by public subscription, it bears the solitary word 'Valour'.

Modern Walsall is well blessed with public parks, one of which – Reedswood – was opened in 1877 and originally consisted of spoil banks from mine workings, a typical example of landscaping former mining sites long before conservation as such was thought about, but it is by no means the most impressive park. To find that, it is necessary to walk a few hundred yards away from the town along Lichfield Street to the Aboretum with its imposing clocktower gateway, beyond doubt the town's pride and joy. It began in 1873 as a business venture when the Walsall

Arboretum and Lake Company was formed to lease a lake and seven acres of land from Lord Hatherton and turn it into a pleasure grounds and gardens. The 'grand opening' took place in 1874, with Lady Hatherton performing the opening ceremony. Admission was not free, but even so, and despite attractions such as a six-day, 600-mile cycle race, the company soon ran into financial difficulties, and in 1884 the council bought the freehold and turned it into a public park. Like Dudley Castle grounds, it became a venue for Whitsuntide fêtes and galas, and it has been extended over the years to cover some eighty acres, making it a first-class amenity with a large boating lake. Its annual illuminations are much acclaimed.

The origin of the Arboretum is of particular interest because it was once the largest of several openwork limestone quarries. Prior to 1824, when Lichfield Street was completed, the road to Lichfield ran across the site, and subsequent worked-out quarries became flooded. This resulted in tragedy when in July 1845 the Mayor of Walsall, John Harvey, was drowned whilst swimming, possibly like many other people under the impression that limestone-impregnated water was beneficial to health. Sadly, a man in a boat also drowned in a rescue bid.

Limestone extraction continued in Walsall until early this century, and a photograph dated around 1900 shows that the underground workings were so vast that horses could be used to haul the tubs of stone. Church Hill is itself undermined, and the late Henry Green, who made a careful study of the town's limestone workings, claimed in 1938 to have been instrumental in discovering an old shaft 'probably made for ventilating the old tunnel workings actually under Church Hill'. It is only a few yards from the steps leading up to St Matthew's, long-since sealed, of course, as are all known entrances to the workings. When Dr Robert Plot wrote in his *Natural History of Staffordshire*, published in 1686, that 'the stone is dug all about Walsall', he was not exaggerating, and for some years into the future Walsall, like Dudley, will face enormous problems in making the area safe. The cost is so prohibitive that help from central government is essential.

One cannot leave Walsall without mention of its football club, which, although not in the same class as its neighbours Wolverhampton Wanderers and West Bromwich Albion, has had its moments. The club was founded in 1888 by the amalgamation of Walsall Swifts, formed in 1877, and Walsall Town, formed two years later, neither of which had made its mark. The new club was tactfully called Walsall Town-Swifts but soon became simply Walsall. The club had the distinction of beating mighty Arsenal 2-0 in the 1933 season and has never forgotten it, although supporters can be fickle. A man who had returned to work after an absence through illness was asked if he had been to see Walsall play. 'No', said he. 'They didn't come to see me when I was bad.'

Walsall town centre has not been sacrificed to traffic but rescued from it, and the ring road is not for the most part purpose-built but follows existing streets, frustrating drivers perhaps but less destructive to property, although some of it is very run down and no doubt improvements will continue to be made. Since we are concerned here with only those parts of Walsall which touch upon the Black Country, there are many suburbs to be excluded. However, one can grab at a vital slice of history by keeping within the north-western part of the borough to visit Bentley (M6 junction 10) where a cairn is all that exists to identify for visitors the site of Bentley Hall.

The story of Charles II's flight after the battle of Worcester in 1651 is often told, and it is here at the end of his trek through the region and out to Boscobel – where he hid in an oak tree – that he arrived as a guest of Colonel Lane. At Bentley the King was virtually inside enemy territory, Staffordshire being under the military governorship of the Parliamentary army, and Jane Lane, sister of Colonel Lane, courageously coaxed a pass from the Governor of Stafford for herself and a servant to go to Bristol. The servant was of course Charles II, his face stained with walnut and his body draped in a plain suit of homespun. In this way he was escorted to safety. After his restoration, the grateful King authorized the Lane coat of arms to incorporate part of the royal arms, specifically three lions from the royal standard. A carved crest of a white horse safely holding the crown topped the arms, whilst below the escutcheon came the Norman-French motto 'Garde le Roy.'

An inn sign outside the Lane Arms at Bentley depicts this coat of arms. Colonel Lane, who could have been buried with honours in Westminster Abbey, chose St Peter's, Wolverhampton, instead and there, as already mentioned, his tomb can be seen.

The imaginative Boscobel legend is common knowledge, at least so we think, but a man sitting in a restaurant overlooking St Peter's towards the end of the 1939-45 war discovered differently. He told me how two fair-haired Americans came up to him and one said, 'Say, sur. How far is it to Notting-ham?' Told about sixty miles, the American explained that they were interested in Robin Hood. 'If you are looking for history,' they were told, 'that church through the window has a thousand years of it, and only six miles from here is Boscobel House where King Charles hid in an oak tree.' The Americans looked puzzled, then the one who hadn't yet spoken said, 'I dig it, sur. The hound of the Boscobels? A guy called Sherlock Holmes?'

They were quickly directed to Nottingham. But we are at Bentley, nicely poised to join the motorway and nip to junction 1 of the M5 at West Bromwich.

7

West Bromwich, Smethwick and Oldbury

Built into the motorway roundabout at the south end of West Bromwich High Street is a relic of Sandwell Hall, an arched stone gateway thought to date from the rebuilding of the hall in about 1711. Sandwell Hall is a suitable place to commence a visit to a town which is the centre of the Metropolitan Borough of Sandwell, the hall being on the site of the medieval priory referred to in Chapter 2. Stebbing Shaw, in his *History of Staffordshire*, 1801, said that some of the priory foundations were traceable in the back part and offices. The hall which rose upon the ruins, and the extensive lands belonging to it, had by the beginning of the eighteenth century come into the possession of the Legge family, later to be earls of Dartmouth, so bringing to the town for close on 250 years a whiff of glorious Devon. Anything more dissimilar can scarcely be imagined.

Sandwell Hall remained the home of the Dartmouths until 1855, by which time the coal and iron industries which they had themselves developed had become too close for comfort, and a move was made to the Shropshire countryside at Patshull, near Albrighton, some eight miles from Wolverhampton. After lying untenanted for a number of years, the hall was put to various uses before being demolished in 1928. The Sandwell Valley Archaeology Project, initiated in 1982, proved Shaw to have been correct, for some walls of the priory were found to have been encased in brick to serve as walls for the hall. Excavations have revealed the remains of priory buildings and of the church belonging to the priory, the remains of a drinking fountain fed by the holy well natural spring (the *sanctus fons* or 'Sanwell' which gave the area its name), and an icehouse used to store ice taken from the pools for use when required for cooling food and drink. Apparently there were two icehouses, the other having been destroyed during the construction of the M5 which cuts clean through the former parklands.

Nature trails have been established to take in the various discoveries, including a haha-type garden boundary consisting of a ditch with a wall on one side, serving as a means of keeping out animals without obstructing the view. There is woodland with many species of trees, a picnic area that once consisted of spoil banks from collieries, and several ponds and lakes. This major conservation area is signposted, with car-parking at Sandwell Park Farm for those wishing to start on one of the trails. At the same time Dartmouth Park, which is incorporated in the scheme, should not be overlooked. Opened in 1878 on land given by Lord Dartmouth, it has all the attributes of a town park and is the venue for various annual events.

The Dartmouths who first came to Sandwell lost no time in exploiting the coal measures and began a major industry that endured in West Bromwich until 1965. The principal pits included Sandwell Colliery, which came into full production in 1877 and petered out early this century, Jubilee Colliery, so called because the first sod was cut in the Diamond Jubilee year of 1897, and the Hamstead Colliery, begun in 1880 and surviving to 1965. Whilst accidents were frequent in all Black Country pits, Hamstead suffered a particularly tragic disaster in 1908 when twenty-six miners were entombed and suffocated, a fact of which I was happily unaware when escorted down in the 1950s and taken five miles underground.

West Bromwich was a late starter industrially despite the distinction of having the first recorded charcoal blast furnace in the Black Country, built in 1590 near the Handsworth boundary by one Thomas Parks – a valuable item of information for which we are indebted to the *Victoria County History, Staffordshire*, Volume 17, which in turn gives the source as the *History of British Iron and Steel* by H.R. Schubert. Also, West Bromwich has moved! Instead of the Domesday settlement of Broomwyche huddled round All Saints Church, the centre of the town is now to the south, occupying an area that until the nineteenth century consisted of heath and woodland. Enclosure of the heath in 1802, quickly followed by a new turnpike road which became part of the main coach road from London to Holyhead, established the present High Street. Here is the town hall of red brick and next to it the central library, opened in 1907 and boldly proclaiming itself a gift by Andrew Carnegie. The High Street is a broad thoroughfare with a number of modern commercial premises and a garden of remembrance fronting the Education Department. Further along, the street is pedestrianized, an expressway to the east serving as a bypass so that there is less hassle and one can actually park – which is how I came to be shown by a schoolboy a small gravestone fronting the pavement and engraved with the solitary letters ET and the date 1833.

Within the pedestrianized zone is the Sandwell Centre, the main shopping area, branching off left and right into Queens Square and Kings Square. Queens Square came first as a joint development between the borough council and the National Coal Board Mineworkers Pension Fund, opened in 1971. A glass case contains a block of Welsh anthracite from an open-cast pit in South Wales. Kings Square, opened three years later, includes a covered market hall. Both squares have unusually designed fountains consisting of curtains of falling water around which is ample seating for the weary. Linked to car-parks and bus station, the whole entity comes as something of a surprise.

The busy expressway has to be crossed to reach the Sandwell Valley Complex and the old parish church which, not surprisingly, is in All Saints Way. The church is mostly nineteenth century with a medieval west tower on which are a sundial and a notice saying that the flagpole was erected in memory of Walter Hackett 1874-1964 (we shall meet him later, p. 112). Inside are monuments to the Whorwoods of Sandwell, to the Dartmouths who succeeded them and to the Turtons of Oak House which we have yet to visit. This remained the only church in West Bromwich until the nineteenth century and today hardly seems to belong to the town, being so far out.

At the commencement of the eighteenth century people lived by following agricultural pursuits, by making nails (sometimes both), by producing metal buckles, until the trade became concentrated in Walsall, or by walking down the hill to Wednesbury where the coal trade was in full swing. Yet by the end of the century firms had become established which exist today: Salter's and Kenrick's are two which are worthy of a closer look.

William Salter started business in Bilston in 1760 with a small weighing device known as a pocket steelyard, and his brother Richard improved it by fashioning a spring out of an old file, thereby not simply producing one of the earliest spring balances but laying the foundations of a huge enterprise. It is not known precisely when the move was made to West Bromwich but development was rapid, and in addition to making all kinds of springs the company made bayonets, a trade which flourished at the time of the Indian Mutiny and during the American Civil War. This company also had an early interest in typewriter-manufacture because it offered an outlet for their small springs, and it is largely due to Salter's that typewriters came to be made locally. By the 1960s Salter's claimed to make a staggering half-million types of springs for innumerable purposes, and there can be few who have not used their bathroom and kitchen scales.

Kenrick's was founded by Archibald Kenrick in 1791, acquiring land in Spon Lane bordering on the canal and erecting a foundry and workshops to make items of domestic ironmongery in cast iron, so beginning a lasting involvement in the holloware industry.

Both companies had in the nineteenth century what is now called a social conscience. Salter's boasted a club with a library, recreation room and dining hall as early as 1859, and even earlier, in 1840, Kenrick's had built a school for the children of employees and others. Known as the Summit School, it was still in existence when the Education Act came into force in 1870 and the school board took over. Kenrick's also gave a park to the town.

To set the seal on social aspects of nineteenth-century industry in West Bromwich, one must return to Salter's for the West Bromwich Albion Football Club began as a Salter works team. At first it was called 'the Strollers' but by 1886 the team had become 'the Albion', and with seven Salter players in the side they played in the final round of the FA cup. Salter's men were to play in the team for more than thirty years, and West Bromwich Albion first won the cup in 1888, beating Preston North End 2-1. Of course the club has won the cup since, and there is always great rivalry between it and the Wolves.

Perhaps we should not dwell overmuch on football, but after all that is what 'West Brom' is best known for among the population generally, and it would not be right to omit mention of its most famous player, Jesse Pennington, even though he last turned out for Albion in 1923. Still remembered, Pennington first played for the club in 1903 at 30 shillings a week. 'Gates averaged five thousand,' he once told me. 'The club couldn't afford 10 shillings for a ton of coke for a hot bath.' Throughout his career he was capped for England no fewer than twenty-five times, a true Black Country hero. Asked how the club got its name 'Throstles' (a throstle – thrush – is depicted on the club badge), he said that in the early days they had a rope instead of a crossbar and one day a thrush landed on it!

As soccer fans will know, Albion's home ground is the Hawthorns, and so famous was this club in 1931, when match attendances were in excess of 35,000, that it was given the distinction of its own railway station or halt, a luxury enjoyed by supporters and visitors for over thirty-five years. Today, at the back of the Hawthorns ground is the start of a 2½-mile parkway/cycle route along a disused railway line. It has been landscaped and for part of its length is a 'trim trail' for joggers.

Swan Village, despite its rural sound, is the site of a giant gasholder and has been since gas was first produced commercially on a large scale. A guide book dated 1838 implied it to be the largest gasworks in the kingdom and 'consequently in the whole world', consuming more than ten thousand tons of coal annually and furnishing more than eighty million cubic feet of gas yearly. The confident assertion that no other country could excel serves to underscore the region's industrial pre-eminence at that time.

Returning to the High Street, one should look in at the library to see the memorial tablet to David Christie Murray, unveiled on 3 December 1908. We have already met Murray in discussing the iniquities of the nail trade against which he fought fiercely in print. Born in the High Street in 1847, he commenced his career on a Wednesbury paper and eventually became a war correspondent, subsequently saying of his home town that it was 'a bald and ugly place, but old association and regard have made it beautiful in my memory for many years'.

By leaving the High Street along Lodge Road between the town hall and Ryland School of Art, one quickly reaches Oak Road. This is not a street-name plucked at random but one rooted – and what word more appropriate! – in the sixteenth century, for here is the truly remarkable Oak House in its garden retreat set unexpectedly amid an estate of council houses. What an incongruous setting it seems for a half-timbered gabled building that has seen off all the terrors and upheavals of the Industrial Revolution to sleep in its 'Old English' garden in which a plaque informs one that John Wesley preached here in 1774.

Oak trees apparently abounded hereabout when the house was built, and the one said to have given the house its name existed in a hollow state until 1846, when it was destroyed by fire. Experts consider the house to consist of three building stages, of which the central hall and side wings are the oldest, the imposing lantern tower being part of the second stage and regarded as extremely rare. The latter stage mainly includes extensions to the rear. The earliest recorded occupiers were the Turtons, a branch of a Lancashire family that came to West Bromwich in about the mid-sixteenth century and were among the first nailors in the vicinity: not any old backyard operators, but traders who became wealthy and gained social distinction. Successive Turtons continued to reside at the Oak House until 1768, when it passed into other hands, until, in 1894, it was purchased for the town by one of its greatest benefactors and first mayor of the borough, Alderman Ruben Farley. He decided to carry out complete restoration and then present it to the town as a museum, which he did in July 1898. Alderman Farley, five times mayor, became West Bromwich's first honorary freeman, and if one continues along the High Street in the direction of Dudley to Carters Green, one comes to a large clocktower erected as a memorial. It includes panels depicting the Oak House and the town hall, and a roundel of himself.

As to the Oak House, it was restored after the 1939-45 war as a Tudor residence and reopened in 1951. Details of its splendid interior and furnishings are best left for the visitor to discover and admire, the building being open to the public, a rural-style treasure in an urban setting.

West Bromwich is extremely lucky to have two buildings of outstanding merit, the rival to the Oak House being the Manor House off Hall Green Road, an even older structure. Although some two miles from the High Street and close to Wednesbury, it is signposted and well worth seeing, having been restored in the early 1960s by the corporation and leased as licensed premises to a brewery company. Extensive restoration work became necessary in the early 1980s, when rotted timber framing was replaced with English oak. Known locally as 'the Old Hall', it is claimed to be one of the most complete examples of a medieval timber-framed building to survive, consisting of a great hall, a north solar wing, a first-floor family chapel and a kitchen block. The whole is surrounded by a moat and approached through a seventeenth-century gatehouse said to be similar to that of Stokesay Castle. It was in a derelict condition when bought by the corporation in 1950 without any idea that a priceless possession had been acquired, and indeed it was deemed irreparable until an expert convinced the council that they had a rare treasure and restoration was decided upon.

The third West Bromwich building of note to warrant a visit is much more humble for it is the person who lived there that gives it merit. It is Asbury Cottage, Newton Road, and a plaque reveals it to have been the home of Francis Asbury (1745-1816), 'The Prophet of the Long Road' who was sent to America by John Wesley in 1771 and became the first bishop of the American Methodist Church. The cottage is dedicated to his perpetual remembrance in association with the World Methodist Council after restoration in 1959. So here is something to bring American tourists further north than Stratford-upon-Avon or 'War-wick'.

The significance of the little cottage is that Asbury's parents moved there soon after he was born and that throughout his life it was to be his only real home, for as an adult he was always on the move or in rented accommodation. He became interested in Methodism at an early age and whilst in his twenties preached throughout the Midland counties. When he heard that Wesley wanted someone to preach in North America, he volunteered, never to return to England. During his forty-five-year ministry in America, he covered an estimated 275,000 miles, mostly on horseback, fighting the elements, poverty and disease and working hard for the 'emancipation of the blacks'. He never married, nor did he become an American citizen in a legal sense, and when he agreed to become the first Methodist bishop, he greatly upset Wesley, who wrote in the strongest terms: 'How can you ... how dare you, suffer yourself to be called bishop?' But Asbury remained undeterred. In 1924 President Calvin Coolidge was present at the unveiling of an equestrian statue of Asbury in Washington DC, paying the Black Country man tribute as one of the builders of the American nation. It is hardly surprising that Asbury is better known across the Atlantic than in the region of his birth.

Another man of West Bromwich destined to make an impact on religious life was John Blackham (1834-1923), credited with having 'discovered' Sunday afternoon. He joined the Ebenezer Congregational Church, became a deacon at the age of twenty-nine and in 1875 founded what became known as the Pleasant Sunday Afternoon Movement, the name originating when he was told by a group of young men that they had nothing against the Bible but why did the sermons in church need to be so dull? Henceforth Blackham decided to use the word 'pleasant' when describing his sermons. His movement flourished until 1908 when it became embodied in another movement.

A few years after John Blackham was born, in 1837, a retail chemist in West Bromwich made a mark of a very different kind when he became engaged on a pioneer project which in more sophisticated forms has enriched the lives of womenfolk ever since (menfolk too if one wants to be feminist!). His name was Hudson, and he started to make in a small way what he called 'dry soap', unexpectedly launching himself on a career that was to make his name literally a household word, for Hudson's, as he called his preparation, was to become synonymous with soap powder. Like many inventions, it was slow to catch on, and by 1854 only ten girls were employed in manufacture. It was another twenty years before he decided to erect a purpose-built factory, and when he did so it was not in his home town but in Liverpool. Hudson's soap was made at both places until the West Bromwich factory closed in 1935. When Hudson died, in 1884, he left the business in trust for his children for six years, after which R.W. Hudson became the proprietor. In 1908 the business was acquired by Lever Brothers, Port Sunlight, Cheshire, and it is thought that Hudson's soap continued to be marketed in some form until 1978, when it was superseded by other brand lines. Few West Bromwich people are aware that the era of washing powder dawned in their High Street.

Brief mention should be made of two other widely contrasting West Bromwich personalities before heading in the direction of the canal system towards Smethwick and the extremity of the Black Country. For one of the characters it is necessary to go back to the early seventeenth century, when one Walter Parsons, a giant of such height as to be described variously as between seven foot six and nine foot (suggestive of elastic tape measures), by virtue of his unusual attributes was made a porter at the Court of James I, a somewhat doubtful honour extending into the reign of Charles I.

More recently and certainly more daintily, West Bromwich is the birthplace of actress Madeleine Carroll, born in 1906 and educated at a local secondary school before moving on to Birmingham University, making her film début in 1928. Her best-known films are *The Thirty Nine Steps* (1935) and *Prisoner of Zenda* (1937). She retired from films in 1949.

The canal system between West Bromwich and Smethwick presents the visitor with the most contrasting and historically renowned features on British waterways, spelling out in visual detail the developments of canal construction in the heart of the industrialized Black Country. For here, separating and rejoicing in the space of a few miles, are the meandering 'Old Main Line' canal and the straight 'New Main Line' opened in 1829. The 'straightness' was achieved by spectacular deep cuttings with towpaths on both sides to facilitate traffic movement at a time when hundreds of narrow boats a day would be using the canal. This whole section is rich in engineering achievement and at one point the old canal is crossed over by means of an aqueduct; here it is possible to glimpse both canal systems, the electrified railway line and the M5 motorway, a living slice of some two hundred years of transport history.

The bridges along this stretch are of outstanding interest, particularly Galton Bridge, built in the late 1820s and the largest canal bridge in the world at that time, having a span of 150 feet. Close to it, so close that if one stands facing the canal on the verge of the busy Telford Way it is impossible to see daylight between the two spans, is the Summit Bridge built by John Smeaton in 1790 when he was modifying the original Brindley line. The next bridge, the blue-brick Brasshouse Bridge, is perhaps as far as we should venture without stepping into Birmingham territory, yet it would be a pity to omit mention of the next one, the Engine Arm Aqueduct of 1825, taking its name from one of the first pumping engines to be built by James Watt and installed nearby in 1770. Happily, it is stored at the Birmingham Science Museum.

The most famous of the inland waterway carrying companies was started in West Bromwich in 1837 by James Fellows. Everyone with a knowledge of canals will be aware of Fellows, Morton & Clayton, the resultant company which lasted until 1948 as perhaps the biggest of all commercial waterway carriers. At one time they operated more than two hundred boats familiarly known as 'Joshers' after Joshua Fellows, but now there is no commercial traffic and the waterways are largely deserted, although the stretch mentioned above is designated the Galton Valley Towing Path Walk with access at Spon Lane, Galton Bridge and Brasshouse Lane.

As for Smethwick, or rather that part of it that concerns us here, West Smethwick as far as the Blue Gates public house in the High Street lacks remarkable features. In fact, the east side of the High Street has been demolished and indeed the area has an appearance of having been peeled of buildings to cater for major roads, one of which runs parallel with the former main road and is crossed by an outsize footbridge. On the western side down-at-heel shops vie for trade with a smallish modern shopping precinct. The whole comes as a shock to a Black Country person who has not had occasion to pass that way since, say, the mid-1970s, and one wonders where all the inhabitants have gone, including the large Asian and Afro-Caribbean community. The answer for the most part is high-rise flats and grids of Victorian streets.

Although Smethwick is recorded in Domesday ('Smedewich'), it appears to have been of little note for hundreds of years and did not even boast a church until the early eighteenth century; in 1801 the population was barely eleven hundred. The arrival of the canal and the railway and the growth of numerous firms of lasting fame resulted in a rise in the population to over 54,000 in 1901, reaching its peak of over 84,000 in the early 1930s. Truly it is born of and belongs to industry.

West Smethwick is not the best of Smethwick, and whilst it is as far as we go, one has to be fair and stress its fine council house with clock turret, its many parks, social amenities and shopping areas. Some of its most renowned industries are too close to Birmingham for mention here, but one cannot ignore Chance Brothers, since its tentacles spread from Smethwick to West Bromwich and it has a history dating to 1814. Now part of the Pilkington Group, it was the first company in England to make sheet glass (1832) and moreover was the only company for close on fifty years to manufacture optical glass, just as there was a time when complete lighthouses were built. Not least, Chance Brothers supplied a $1\frac{1}{4}$ million square feet of glass for the Crystal Palace built for the Great Exhibition of 1851. All in all a marvellous record of achievement in which Black Country workers played their part in peace and war.

If one leaves Smethwick via the West Park (a gift of a member of the Chance family in 1896), one comes to the oddly sounding district of Rood End and can easily take a side glance at Tat Bank, not an endearing name, for 'tat' in the local idiom is junk and those who collect it are 'tatters'. However, adjacent Popes Lane does give a sort of uplift, and hereabout is the giant British Industrial Plastics Company which dates to 1894 and was formed to develop the production of cyanide for no other reason than that, shortly before, the gold-mining countries of the world had begun to use cyanide for the extraction of gold from low-grade ores. Subsequently BIP became pioneers in the plastics industry. However, it was not the first chemical works to develop in this heavily industrialized area of Oldbury which we have now reached. In so doing we have crossed from traditional Staffordshire into traditional Worcestershire, and just to make it even more confusing, Oldbury was a detached part of Shropshire from the thirteenth century, when it had links with Halesowen Abbey. Oldbury was to gain the status of a municipal borough in 1935 but oh dear what of it now? The former town centre is one vast supermarket/car park complex with the old town hall clinging resolutely to one corner. Landscaping and war memorial complete the central area, the road towards Birmingham consisting of decaying properties and a hemmed-in nineteenth-century church is in what is planned as a conservation area. There seems much to be done!

A First World War tank used to stand in the market-place as a reminder that the very first tank was made at the Metropolitan Carriage Works then located within the urban district of Oldbury. This fact might be challenged by other tank-manufacturers but the evidence is sound enough, for seven thousand peace celebration medals struck in 1919 for local schoolchildren not only depict the tank but were actually made from tank salvage material donated by the firm.

Oldbury is the home of one of the country's most important tube-producers, Accles & Pollock, established to make cycle tubes in 1902 and credited with many 'firsts' – the first to make streamlined tube for aircraft (1910), the first to produce a tubular steel golf shaft (1913 but not accepted by the golfing fraternity until 1929) and so on down the years. The company's guiding light until the 1950s was Walter Hackett CBE (1874-1964), whose name appears on the tower of All Saints Church, West Bromwich. He had a life-long habit of corresponding and commenting on events in verse under the name 'Khanyer Whackett' and had a fine sense of humour as well as a shrewd business head. Fond of relating everyday stories of working folk, he often told how in the early days at Oldbury he asked a workman to sort out four different sizes of tube, only to be told when the job was done: 'Gaffer, them's the little 'uns, them's the big 'uns, them's the big little 'uns and them's the little big 'uns.'

As has been indicated, Black Country humour can be absurd ('I told yer to build a chimney an' yo'n built a well' – 'Arr, we'd got the plans upside down') but what happened for real at Bromford Road, Oldbury, in 1984 is more ridiculous than anything a local might come up with. It was the opening of British Rail's brand new main line station 'Sandwell and Dudley', a name insisted upon despite vigorous protest by interested organizations who rightly maintained that, since it is in Oldbury, it should be called Oldbury Station. As a result visitors alight at the station under the impression that they are in Dudley, which is some three miles away, or at Sandwell, which is a vast Metropolitan Borough, has no town of that name and virtually means West Bromwich, a mile distant. It is doubtless assumed that people will get used to it in time, but hard luck on strangers!

Black Country towns do not lend themselves to incorporation in song. 'By the Time I Get to Bilston', 'Wolverhampton, My Home Town' and 'April in Netherton' do not trip readily off the tongue, so it is not surprising that, when Jack Judge wrote his most famous and enduring song, he should look elsewhere for a town to pin it on. He chose 'Tipperary'. Jack Judge was born in 1872 in a poor part of Oldbury, starting working life at the age of nine, and five years later found himself pushing a fishmonger's barrow. From entertaining the crowds in the market-place with his rhyming and singing, he became a popular music hall artist and went on tour. It was whilst he was appearing at Stalybridge, Cheshire, that, so the story goes, he made a bet that he could write and produce a song in one night. He won his bet by singing that same night, 31 January 1912, 'It's a Long Way to Tipperary'. It must be said that his claim is disputed by those who say that a Warwickshire man named Harry Williams, who sometimes worked with Judge, was the originator of the song, but the latter's claim is certainly the stronger, for on 31 January 1953 a memorial tablet was unveiled at Stalybridge. It reads:

Remembering with Pride
   Jack Judge
   who in this street and building
   was inspired to write and compose
   the immortal marching song ...
   It's A Long Way To Tipperary
He was also the first to sing it in public in the Grand Theatre opposite, 31 January 1912.

The unveiling was carried out by no less a celebrity than the late band-leader/impresario Jack Hylton, in the presence of Jack Judge's brother Ted, for Jack had died in 1938 and is buried in Rood End cemetery.

   Oldbury has an historical connection with commerce for Lloyd's Bank set up their first branch there in 1864, apparently for no other reason than to save one of its best industrial customers from having to send a coach to Birmingham to collect money for wages. The premises, 30 Birmingham Street, are still occupied by the bank. That apart, Oldbury remains, despite the recession, a sprawl of factories in which the chemical industries have a notable role. It is hardly a place in which to linger, but it is fitting that one leaves with a reminder of the canals and motorways which in their respective era so transformed the environment. These contrasting systems can be seen to good effect at Titford Canal and Pools, restored and landscaped in the 1970s. Here it is possible to gaze upon long stretches of sparkling water and look up at the awesome stilted road of the motorway network. Access is alongside the New Navigation public house on the Birmingham-Wolverhampton New Road close to M5 junction 2.

8

Wednesbury, Darlaston and Willenhall

Wednesbury played an important role in the industrial development of the Black Country, being the earliest volume coal-mining centre in the region and, as we have seen, the first town to benefit commercially by the construction of Brindley's canal. It is easy to pinpoint from the central ridge at places like Dudley by reason of its parish church, which rises above the urban sprawl that covers the gentle slopes of the Tame valley. The blackened church is St Bartholomew's, medieval in origin with a fourteenth-century tower arch, but principally nineteenth-century. It is famed for its unusual lectern, for instead of the usual eagle supporting the Bible on outstretched wings, there is a fighting cock complete with spurs and shaven comb. Considering it is around four hundred years old, it underlines the sustained interest in cock-fighting – said to be an emblem of courage – that existed in the region until the 'sport' was banned at the end of the eighteenth century, although in fact it was to continue for over a hundred years afterwards.

Wednesbury was probably no more involved in cock-fighting than were neighbouring towns and villages but an eighteenth-century ballad, 'The Wednesbury Cocking', has been handed down, positively identifying the town with its prevalence. Far too long to include here in full, it begins:

At Wednesbury there was a cocking
A match between Newton and Scoggins.

The colliers and nailers left work
And all to old Spittles went jogging.
To see this noble sport
Many noble men resorted.
And although they'd little money
With it they freely sported.

The verses go on to relate how rival cock-owners and their
supporters at the main (a term denoting a round) began to fight
among themselves, so that:

It's a wonder no man was slain.
So they trampled both cocks to death
And this made a draw of the main.

St Bartholomew's stands on Church Hill amid a churchyard of
equally blackened tombstones, the hillside now landscaped and
altogether much more open than of old, divided from the town
centre by a major roadway close to where roundabouts on the
northern bypass send traffic on its way without penetrating the
town itself. Offering distant views of urban development, the hill
also accommodates the Roman Catholic Church of St Mary's,
built of brick in the 1870s and having a slender steeple. Here too
is Ethelfleda Terrace, the reason for the name becoming
apparent a short way along where there is a small garden feature
and a plaque which explains that this was the site of 'the graf or
fighting platform of the stronghold built by Ethelfleda, Princess
of Mercia, daughter of King Alfred the Great, about A.D. 916
when she fortified Wednesbury against the Danes'. The garden
was constructed in 1953. At the foot of the hill there stands in
isolation a large redbrick pub called 'The Woden' and close to it
an underpass which takes one into the town, whose street pattern
appears little changed in recent times, although modern housing
has crept close to the centre in Lower High Street. The
market-place retains its square brick clocktower with baroque
stone top, erected by public subscription to commemorate the
coronation of George V in 1911.
   The public buildings in Holyhead Road consist of post office,
adult education centre, town hall and art gallery set in a tight
row, with the Anchor pub tacked on for good measure. The

public library, built in 1908 and described by Pevsner as the best secular building of Wednesbury, stands on the corner of Walsall Street and Hollis Drive. Immediately opposite is a garden of remembrance dedicated in 1926 and again in 1953.

Wednesbury is yet another Domesday location ('Wednesberie') and one more possibly derived from the Saxon god Woden. The market, familiarly known as Wedgbury Market, has a charter dating to 1709, which is very late as markets go hereabouts, but what it lacks in age it makes up for in tradition, losing much of its character when it was moved under cover in Camp Street. The charter also granted two fairs annually, and this led to the custom of walking the fairs, a ritual involving many visits to public houses in the process. By the nineteenth century the town had developed a reputation for disorderly revelry, for the annual wake was formerly abolished in 1874 in an order signed by no less a person than the Home Secretary. However, it continued to be held on private ground until almost the end of the century. What it is to have a reputation whereby forty years earlier it could be said: 'The population scarcely ever thought of anything but eating and drinking when the day's labour was over.'

Industrially, Wednesbury earned for itself the nickname 'Tube Town' following an invention by a local man. An old water-powered ironworks was acquired by one Edward Elwell in about 1817 and converted into steam-powered operation for the manufacture of edge tools, thereby creating a firm of major importance in the future. It was here in 1825 that a workman named Cornelius Whitehouse perfected a method of forging a hollow tube. He realized that, if the strip from which the tube was made could be suitably heated, it could be drawn through a pair of semi-circular dies and so welded. Elwell advised him to take his patent to the proprietor of the Crown Tube Works, as a result of which Whitehouse was employed and given help to patent the invention, destined to revolutionize a trade which had begun to boom when the rapid growth of the gas industry earlier in the century had created widespread demand for wrought-iron tube. When Whitehouse's patent expired in 1844, a number of rival tube firms became established, some to endure for more than a century and subsequently to turn to steel and 'weldless' tubing.

The nineteenth century was not short of inventiveness both nationally and locally, and within a decade of Whitehouse's tube a Nonconformist minister came up with another winner when he thought out an improved type of iron axle for carts. It sounds a trifling thing now but horse-drawn transport was as vital then as is the motor vehicle today, and his patent marked the birth of what was to be one of Wednesbury's greatest companies, the Patent Shaft, referred to locally as 'the Shaft'. Again it was a case of the right product at the right time, for very soon came the railway boom and a switch was made to making railway axles and later wheels. Early this century the company was engaged in steel-making and rolling but in spite of modernization it closed in 1980, to the shock and dismay of the local community.

During its existence the Shaft acquired the ironworks of Lloyd's Foster, which brings us to that same Quaker Lloyd banking family that opened its first branch at Oldbury. Samuel Lloyd joined forces with his brother-in-law Joseph Foster in 1818 and established a company which had the distinction in 1864 of setting up the first Bessemer steel plant to operate in the Midlands. Unfortunately economic factors were to negate this initiative, and the concern went bankrupt three years later, enabling their main competitors, the Shaft, to purchase. The reason Lloyd's Foster went broke was because it lost £$\frac{1}{4}$ million on a contract for the new wrought-iron Blackfriars Bridge, London. By the time this bridge was opened by Queen Victoria in 1869, the company had lost its identity, whilst amalgamation made the Shaft the largest works in the whole of Staffordshire.

The thick coal in the region of Wednesbury was prone to spontaneous combustion, and Dr Plot's note that 'Some coal pits may and do take fire of themselves' was affirmed many times, one of the most disastrous occasions being in 1897 when a road gave way, 'exuding flames as well as smoke in blinding volume'. Barricades were erected and a night watchman was appointed to safeguard the public. One night the watchman left his box to warn approaching men of the danger and somehow fell into one of the burning holes. A brave constable who brought up the body after two attempts was, it is said, awarded a medal by the Prince of Wales. Having claimed its victim, the fire banked down, only to burst forth again later on, so seriously that sewers, gas mains and tramlines were threatened and a sand trench was constructed as a firebreak. The town was saved but underground fires continued spasmodically. Whilst there have been no such outbreaks in modern times, Wednesbury continues to suffer the ravages of mineral extraction, for in February 1985 over 350 homes were at risk from the collapse of limestone workings. It is a continuing problem shared with Dudley and Walsall, and likely to remain so into the foreseeable future.

In addition to its famed industrial base, Wednesbury is the one Black Country town most associated with John Wesley, for although he preached throughout the region with less than enthusiastic response, it is here that he almost met his death. The story of the Wednesbury riots is well known locally, and indeed the Black Country Society in co-operation with the Methodist Philatelic Society issued a special postal cover to mark the 230th anniversary of the riots, which began on 20 October 1743. After Wesley had preached from a horseblock, he went to the home of one of his converts from whence he was forceably taken by a mob to the magistrate, who said 'What do I want with Wesley?' and sent them packing. The men took the preacher to another magistrate without receiving satisfaction so they dragged him back to the town, during which 'I talked all the time to those within hearing,' Wesley said later. Apparently his demeanour impressed some of his attackers and they softened towards him, one George Clifton, a 'rough collier', being credited with saving the preacher's life, carrying him on his back over a stream to safety. The homes and property of local Methodists were attacked the following February during what became known as the Shrovetide Riots, the Wednesbury mob being joined by those from neighbouring areas. Considering such antagonism, it is surprising that Methodism became strongly rooted throughout the Black Country.

Industrialists also played their part in furthering religious causes, and as evidence one can look to the Elwells, already mentioned as the proprietors of Wednesbury Forge, part of which still exists under another name. Here at Wood Green, a pleasant residential area beyond Brunswick Park, stands St Paul's church, 'built to the greater glory of God and in memory of their father and grandfather late of the Forge, Wood Green ... by Edward, Henry, Alfred and Frederick Elwell'. Dedicated in August 1874, it is described as being in the thirteenth-century or

Early Geometrical style and was paid for totally by the Elwell family, less a small grant by the Lichfield Diocesan Church Building Fund. The tower and 125-foot spire were completed in 1887.

To venture from the church across the nearby motorway junction is to arrive at Bescot, where we have been before, so it is necessary to take one of those busy roads at the foot of Church Hill to Darlaston, a mile distant.

Having left Wednesbury at a link between church and industry, it does not come amiss to enter Darlaston quoting another example, for All Saints' Church is connected with the first blast furnace there on a site where ironmaking is thought to have taken place in the seventeenth century. The furnace was under the proprietorship of two men of like-sounding names, Bills and Mills. When the latter died, in 1806, his widow married the other partner, and Mills' only son Samuel ultimately became proprietor of the Darlaston Green Furnaces and a man of wealth, some of which his widow used to build a church to his memory, this being the first All Saints' erected and consecrated in 1872. It was destroyed by enemy action in July 1942 and a descendant of the Mills family laid the foundation stone of the present church in 1952.

Darlaston must have been embodied in surrounding manors at the time of Domesday, for it is not mentioned in the Survey and seems to have been kicked around quite a bit thereafter, for little is known until the Hearth Tax of 1665 reveals Darlaston as consisting of 145 households. Whilst it is thought that the first church at Darlaston was built around the thirteenth century, there is no proof and the first parish church of St Lawrence was built in the seventeenth century, enlarged in 1721, then rebuilt in brick in 1807. The present church is nineteenth-century with its tower and spire as late as 1907.

Mining became prevalent here in the eighteenth century, and despite participation by colliers in the Wesley riots, a Methodist meeting house had appeared by the early 1760s, replaced by a new building in 1810. This has been demolished and the site occupied by a housing development known as Wesley Fold. But the town did not become alive industrially until the growth of the gunmaking trade which it shared with Wednesbury and, to a lesser extent, with West Bromwich and Wolverhampton. The year 1754 was one of peak demand when Birmingham gunsmiths grasped at every gunlock, gun barrel and item of 'smallwork' the Black Country towns could supply. It is ironic that in a region of economic slavery local skills were employed to assist in the purchase of African slaves, guns being a major item of 'currency'. The gun was Darlaston's main export, and in fact so urgent was demand that for a time Birmingham manufacturers were willing to pay over the odds so that those skilled in gunmaking must have felt themselves to be in clover. Perhaps they grew careless, greedy or both, for word got around that the guns were poorly finished and like as not to kill whoever first fired them. Yet a gunlock filer needs a five-year apprenticeship to develop skills in filing the small components of a gunlock mechanism. When the slave trade was abolished, it spelt doom for Darlaston, or so it appeared, but freed of pressing demand the trade settled down to produce fine guns, often with elaborate scrollwork, until well into the present century.

English Gunmakers by de Witt Bailey and Douglas A. Nie gives Darlaston as being the earliest to have developed the gun trade, with over three hundred gunlock filers, more than fifty gunlock forgers, and with 250 boys engaged as lock forgers and filers in the mid-eighteenth century. During the next century seventy-seven makers are listed, many being in the same family – for example, Spittle of 'Wednesbury Cocking' fame appears ten times, and Cornelius Whitehouse, renowned for his technique of forging a hollow tube, is listed as a gun barrel maker. One Darlaston man combined his gun business with that of butcher, doubtless with unconscious irony! Bills and Mills are there as well as one Thomas Rubery, which brings us nicely to one of the two names of a giant company that was to put Darlaston on the map worldwide and have immense ramifications across a whole range of modern industries – Rubery Owen. In 1893 John Tunner Rubery formed a partnership with Alfred Ernest Owen in the management of a light steel construction company which entered the cycle boom and went on to triumph in the motor industry and aviation.

Darlaston is still the headquarters of Rubery Owen, with international interests, although falling demand from the automotive industry led to the closure of the main component factories at Booth Street in the early 1980s. It was a sad blow to the area, but the company soldiers on in other fields.

As with guns, Darlaston was a forerunner of the bolt and nut industry, and in Bilston museum is an 'English Oliver', the first bolt-forming machine, attributed to Thomas Oliver of Darlaston, who, it is claimed, was the originator of the bolt and nut industry in England. By 1860 there were eight major factories in the trade along with many smaller establishments.

When I was a child, certain elderly relatives would use the expression 'silly juggins' to describe someone who had committed a stupid deed, and it was not until some fifty years later that I discovered that juggins was a person! In fact, Richard Juggins, born in Darlaston in 1843 and apprenticed to a nut and bolt maker, became in the 1880s combined secretary of the Nut and Bolt Makers Association and the Gunlock Filers Association. He instigated the coming together of various small Black Country unions as the Midland Counties Trades Federation, formed in 1873, and thereafter, as its secretary, wielded considerable influence. In that capacity he became involved in strike action over attempts to reduce prices during a time of recession and ultimately suggested the setting-up of a wages board for the industry: it came into being in 1889. Juggins died six years later, by which time my elders, who tended to side with employers, had undoubtedly picked up the 'silly' tag early in life. 'The working man will be the ruination of this country,' remained one of their pet sayings to the end of their days.

King Street has been Darlaston's principal thoroughfare for some three hundred years and before taking on the role of shopping centre contained the houses of influential people. One such was a building called Poplar House, and here in about 1860 whilst staying with relatives Mrs Henry Wood, the famous Victorian novelist, wrote *East Lynne*. A plaque tells the story.

With the growth of its specialized industries Darlaston became a thriving town, but here there is a story of twentieth-century decline because by the 1960s movement of population to new housing estates had resulted in shop closures until fears were publicly expressed that the town was doomed and local people who cared began to fight for something to be done to preserve their town. The arrival of a supermarket halted the decline, and now a modern town has emerged, King Street being a neatly paved area with new shop premises and a twice weekly market.

The main historic feature here is represented in the form of a symbolic bull stake. Again one reads a plaque for the details:

From the seventeenth century or earlier the area around the Bull Stake was the main focal point of the town of Darlaston.

The Bull Stake itself was originally a few feet south west of its present position, and was used until Victorian times in connection with the popular blood sports of bull and bear baiting.

Although bull-baiting was declared illegal in 1825, the cruel sport continued for some years regardless of the clergy and like-minded folk who tried to stamp it out.

Church Street, a shopping continuation of King Street, brings us to the church of St Lawrence, seemingly of no great distinction although one is attracted – staggered is probably a better word – by the monstrously oversize statue of a mother and child erected in the churchyard in 1958 with no indication of the sculptor's identity. The churchyard was dedicated as a garden of rest in 1954, and the lychgate is inscribed to the memory of Councillor Alfred Ernest Owen, 'benefactor of the town and parish of St Lawrence', dated 1943.

The Owen family, whose once vast works have been mentioned, are much revered in Darlaston, and by continuing along Church Street past a modern Catholic Church and the 'Why Not' public house, one arrives at the Green, once the site of fairs and games but not truly a green for many generations until the demolition of St George's Church returned it to at least a rest-garden area. This church lasted 123 years (1852-1975), and not only were various members of the Owen family churchwardens but after demolition employees at the Owen works took it upon themselves to rescue the stone pulpit and other worthwhile relics for which they found homes elsewhere. On a corner here stands a sculpture of St George and the Dragon erected in 1954.

There is a considerable amount of modern housing hereabouts, an encouraging sight for those who had feared a deserted town, and two parks, Victoria Park and George Rose Park, the former taking in the grounds of Darlaston House, the family home of the Mills, the town's first ironmasters. Until the 1960s it was divided by a railway, and whilst various road bridges remain the lines have been taken up to make a leisure walkway. The George Rose

Park dates to 1924 and is named after a bolt and nut manufacturer. Its ornamental wrought-iron gates remain, having somehow escaped the wartime drive for scrap metal.

Darlaston offers nothing more to keep one from progressing from the Green for about a mile into Willenhall, traditional centre of lockmaking: not gunlocks but security locks of all kinds.

Willenhall, the 'Winehale' of Domesday, is a name synonymous with locks, and it *shows*! Lockmaking companies encroach on the town itself, and one has only to peer from the main thoroughfare, Stafford Street (partly pedestrianized), down either Wood Street or Union Street to see factory building housing world leaders in the trade. Locks have been made here since the sixteenth century, mostly of wood until the iron trade got into its stride locally, and even then they tended to be designed for ornament rather than security. At first Wolverhampton claimed to have made a greater input to the trade but by the mid-nineteenth century Willenhall's tally of locksmiths had a lead over Wolverhampton of about two to one.

Before the advent of the factory system, lockmaking was a cottage industry carried out by skilled craftsmen assisted by their families. Apprentices, often drawn from workhouses at about the age of ten, lived with the family and were harshly treated, working as much as sixteen hours a day in tiny workshops with a minimum of nourishing food. This led to the town gaining a reputation as being the cruellest in the country, and an early nineteenth-century account declared that, 'In Willenhall the children are beaten shamefully with horsewhip, strap, stick, hammer, hammer handle, file or whatever tool is nearest at hand.'

Whatever the truth of the matter, there can be no denying the skill of those early locksmiths, using only simple tools. One of the earliest factories appeared in 1790 and endured in one form or another until the 1980s, beginning a system whereby instead of working at home the men assembled at a given place for a specific number of hours. Even so, it remained largely a handcraft industry, the first steam-hammer for forging appearing in 1856. Many firms of lasting reputation developed, the two giants being Josiah Parkes and Yale. Of these, Parkes' was founded in 1840 and traded as iron-merchants before switching to locks in 1896, a milestone being the introduction of the cylinder locks in 1911.

When I said I was going to Yale, someone said, 'Locks or university?' I couldn't find a university in Willenhall so I visited the lock firm and found that it does in fact tie in with the continent that has the famed university, for in 1868 one Linus Yale invented in America the modern pin tumbler lock which utilizes a small flat key, ideal for mass production. Yale arrived in Willenhall in 1929, when they bought out an established lock company. Today these companies and others have turned lock-production into an assembly line process which places them more in the realm of light engineers than skilled craftsmen, though inherent skills do exist. All the same, it is a far cry from the days when the lock filer became permanently stooped through years at the workbench and earned for Willenhall the nickname 'Umpshire' by reason of the many humpbacked inhabitants. There is a tale that public houses had holes cut into the wall behind the benches to receive the humps of the men when they came in for their pint. The niceties of ignoring infirmity were never a strong feature in the Black Country!

Before leaving the fascinating subject of locks, so essential in these crime-ridden times that demand is high and Willenhall produces about ninety per cent of requirements, mention must be made of the town's lock museums, that adjoining the public library in Walsall Street which houses a static display of locally-made locks, and the 'independent' National Lock Museum in New Road, opened in mid-1985. The latter comprises a locksmith's house and a group of workshops complete with nineteenth-century equipment. They were continually occupied by lockmakers since the 1840s and when the last resident locksmith died in 1972 the workshops were closed and left to posterity.

This important 'living' museum, maintained by a trust, is concerned with the lock industry of today as well as that of the past, so that modern security systems can be seen, including those embodying electronics. Local craftsmen demonstrate their skills and a strong educational commitment is foreseen. It is hoped that eventually 'visitors will be able to serve mini one-day or half-day 'apprenticeships' and walk away with a lock they have made themselves.'

Those same visitors will be surprised to see a lock museum fronted by a restored Victorian draper's shop, but this is how this particular family augmented the locksmith's trade, giving the females in the household a chance to participate gainfully.

Such restored premises apart, Willenhall has no buildings of historic interest, doubtless because a 'great fire' in the seventeenth century destroyed the Tudor residences and spared them the indignity of mines and ironworks already in the offing. The population is estimated at 350 in 1690 and just over a thousand by 1801, so clearly there was no major influx of labour: a different story a century later when the population exceeded eighteen thousand. The town was not designated a parish in its own right until 1840, prior to which the church of St Giles in Walsall Street was a chapel under the jurisdiction of Wolverhampton, a fact which would not have pleased independent locals. The present St Giles is nineteenth-century, the third to be built there and named after the patron saint of cripples – not by reason of those humpbacked locksmiths but because of a healing well.

A large stone sculpture of a lock, sited just off the market-place on the forecourt to commercial premises, bears a number of weatherbeaten plaques, one of which reads: 'A certain well near Spring Lane was reputed to possess healing properties and in 1726 on a stone near the well an inscription read: This spring has of long been celebrated for healing of morbid conditions of the eyes and skin.'

This same stone sculpture carries the following homily around its base: 'He who loseth the key to his treasure maketh the locksmith to labour in vain.' And that's not all, for there are indistinct outlines of tokens as reminders of a time when coins of small denominations were not minted and traders issued their own tokens until they were made illegal in 1867. Among the last tokens to be issued in Willenhall were farthings, one in particular showing on the obverse a padlock, curry comb and door bolt, with the word 'Let Willenhall Flourish' and dated 1844. The other side bears the name of the supplier John Austin who combined the trades of miller, baker and grocer.

Whilst the aforementioned spring many have possessed healing properties, it was of little use in 1849, when cholera struck so severely that, the churchyard being full, unconsecrated ground known as Doctor's Piece was used as a burial ground. From August to October there were 292 deaths from the plague, 211 being buried in Doctor's Piece. Still known as such, it is now enclosed as a memorial garden.

Doctor's Piece had belonged to the town's most revered son, Dr Richard Wilkes (1690-1760), antiquary, diarist, parson, doctor of medicine and an all-round good egg despite apparently practising medicine without a licence. He is credited with getting the medieval church demolished and a replacement built in about 1750. One wonders what he would have thought of the church's notorious nineteenth-century parson, a fellow named Moreton, who was described as a rum-sodden sot who loved blood sports and prompted outsiders to chant:

A tumbledown church,
A tottering steeple,
A drunken parson
And a wicked people.

The most attractive feature of the market-place, along which stalls align despite attempts during the last century to drive them under cover, is an elaborate stone clocktower erected to the memory of Joseph Tonks by the Friendly Societies of Willenhall and his fellow townsmen, 10 May 1892. Dr Tonks must have been highly regarded or else the town badly wanted a belated rival to Sister Dora in neighbouring Walsall. The stone and ironwork of the clock were restored in 1979, the fountains and basins being original.

9

Halesowen, the Cradleys and Old Hill

Halesowen lies in a valley close to the foot of the thousand foot-high Clent Hills, separated from this noted beauty spot by the same bypass that divides it from the ruins of its thirteenth-century abbey, which is to the east of the Bromsgrove Road. At the time of Domesday it was called 'Hala' and was held by Roger Montgomery, Earl of Shrewsbury. This resulted in the manor being in Shropshire, and incredibly the town continued to be a detached part of that county for almost eight hundred years, until it came under Worcestershire once again in 1844.

Hala had changed to Hales when it was granted by Henry II to David ap Owen, Prince of Wales, in 1177 and thus became known as Hales Owen. It is still spelt as two words by purists and appears thus on the letterheads of certain firms' stationery. When Owen died, in 1204, the manor reverted to the Crown, and King John bestowed it on the Bishop of Winchester, who gave it to the Premonstratensian canons to form an abbey, which they did in 1214. The abbot was responsible for Halesowen being made a borough in about 1232, a distinction it retained until it found itself omitted from the Municipal Reform Act of 1835. Borough status was regained in 1936, but alas for civic pride, all was lost when it was absorbed into Dudley in 1974. At the time the peeved authority issued a booklet with the title *Last Will and Testament*, placing on record the borough's achievements.

The town centre is largely modern and precincted, blending well with the older streets adjacent and still happily dominated by the parish church of St John the Baptist, founded on the site of a Saxon church by Roger de Montgomery, believed to have fought at Hastings. There is considerable Norman work including the nave arches, west wall and very large font with figures at the corners mounted on pillars. The building embodies a mixture of fourteenth/fifteenth-century work, said to account for the unusual position of the tower, closer to the west end of the structure than to the east. The tall grey spire is less noticeable than of old because of modern office blocks and flats, but seen across gardens as one enters the town from the Birmingham side it looks very fine. Until 1882 the curfew was rung, the bell tolling for several minutes, then lowered and tolled the number to correspond with the day of the month, prompting one to imagine Dad yelling to his family: 'Shurrup and listen to what day it is.'

Reconstruction of the church again took place in the nineteenth century, and its re-opening in 1884 coincided with the birth of Halesowen's most famous son, to whom, fittingly, there is a commemorative plaque in the church – Francis Brett Young. He was the son of Dr Thomas Brett Young, the town's first medical officer of health as well as a GP, a most respected man of his day and a churchwarden from 1903 to 1905. Francis also qualified as a doctor, but after service in the Royal Medical Corps in South Africa under General Smuts and being invalided out as disabled from malaria, he turned to writing and produced a string of novels set in the Midlands, changing the names of towns and geographical features so that his native town became Halesby, Wolverhampton Wolverbury, Dudley Dulston and so on. Although he wrote novels based in South Africa where he lived later in life, his Black Country ones are of particular interest, for he understood not only the ironmasters but the colliers and ironworkers he had seen in his father's surgery. The Black Country novels, published between 1916 and 1938, include what is probably his best-known work, *My Brother Jonathan*, set in Wednesford (Wednesbury), for it has been filmed twice as well as televised, although the visual medium cannot convey his vivid descriptive prose nor can actors interpret the true inflections of the dialect.

Brett Young is not regarded as a first-rank novelist, but in 1950 Birmingham University, where he had obtained his medical degree, did go so far as to confer upon him a honorary degree, Doctor of Letters, in recognition of his contribution to literature. Brett Young died in 1954, his birthplace 'The Laurels' was demolished, and very few of his total of over thirty works are still in print. Today's loyal readers regard him as underrated, and in 1979 the Brett Young Society was formed, organizing a series of commemorative events during his centenary year of 1984.

Halesowen boasts a much earlier literary figure considerably wider known but now generally regarded as falling into the category of a minor poet – William Shenstone (1714-63). In his lifetime Shenstone received considerable acclaim, his works running to as many as thirty editions even in the nineteenth century, whilst he became almost as well known as a landscape gardener, transposing his birthplace, 'The Leasowes' ('Lezzers' to Black Country folk), into one of the most celebrated pleasure gardens of his time, visited by people of eminence such as Doctor Johnson and Oliver Goldsmith – possibly even by Lord Byron, as well as by the aristocracy staying at Hagley Hall, some three miles to the west, home of the Littelton family who themselves played a role in the development of the area.

To find 'The Leasowes' one leaves the town to tackle Mucklow Hill, a road rising from the valley to over four hundred feet leading on to the Birmingham plateau at Quinton, once narrow and tree-lined but now a dual carriageway with industrial estates on both sides of its lower slopes. Still treacherous in winter, it is no longer necessary for passengers to alight from buses and walk so that the vehicle can climb the 1 in 8 section. The entrance to 'The Leasowes' is on the right as one climbs, down a short lane signposted 'Leisure Park' to a large car-park. In recent years the grounds have been re-organized and a trail has been marked to enable visitors to take in such surviving features as a ruinated priory, inscribed seats, urns and special trees. Shenstone had a 'natural' approach to landscaping and made imaginative use of existing streams, though his so-called miniature Niagara cascade is no more. Close to the car-park is a short stretch of canal that leads nowhere yet is actually part of a once thriving artery of commerce which came down from the Netherton Tunnel and continued beyond 'The Leasowes' to join the Birmingham Canal at Selly Oak. In so doing it passed outside the Black Country through Lapal Tunnel, in its day the fourth longest canal tunnel in Britain, its usefulness to commercial traffic being prematurely curtailed in 1917 due to mining subsidence.

Also close to the car-park is a children's playground, and there is an explanatory map listing the highlights offered by a walk in the still extensive grounds, part utilized as a golf course although the golf house is not the original Shenstone home but a replacement built in 1776 and much altered. Shenstone left to posterity something of his boyhood Halesowen in his work 'The Schoolmistress', in which he portrays the dame of his old school, one Sarah Lloyd, who is believed to have been in her fifties when he attended her thatched cottage-cum-school. Shenstone left for Oxford in 1732 and did not return to 'The Leasowes' until some ten years later, so that his oft-quoted 'Lines Written to an Inn' have nothing to do with the Black Country.

Who'er has travell'd life's dull round,
Where'er his stages may have been,
May sigh to think he still has found
The warmest welcome at an inn.

The poet is buried in Halesowen churchyard, where also are the remains of an ancient cross which once stood in what is known as Great Cornbow, location of the town's first 'constabulary station'. The cross was blown down in a gale in 1908 and rescued from a rubbish tip by what we would now term a conservationist.

Halesowen's traffic-free centre retains the old names, such as Peckingham Street leading to Birmingham Street once busy with factories but now largely given over to open-air car-parks. A plaque in the precinct tells us that the Leconstoone brook divided High Street from Hagley Street and that the bridge needed repair in 1485. There is no sign of it today – and what an odd name for a brook anyway! Along Hagley Street past Great Cornbow an entertainment centre replaces the borough hall (now used by industry) which served the town's social needs for many a decade.

Overall, Halesowen is more rural in aspect than other fringe Black Country towns, still retaining some half-timbered houses in Church Street and with well-kept gardens, parks and playing fields, bordered in the south-west by open countryside against a backdrop of the Clent Hills. Even so, there is a considerable variety of industries, and its industrial heritage is strong. The weaving and fulling of cloth were an early involvement followed by a massive incursion into nail-making, which is why an anvil forms part of the town's coat of arms. An anonymous scribe wrote in 1844: 'In the midst of God's bounty and loveliness stalks the curse of poverty – the whole population of this beauteous region being, without distinction of sex, nailors, a name at once descriptive of all poverty and wretchedness.'

In truth the plight of the Halesowen nailors cannot have differed greatly from that of those in neighbouring towns. A nineteenth-century account records that they had to walk three miles to fetch iron and worked 109 hours a week for 1½d. an hour. Small wonder that strikes were frequent. In 1846 upwards of four hundred nail-forgers were on strike, a highlight of unrest occurring on 18 February 1852 when nailmakers from all over the region assembled to draw a wagon load of coal from Halesowen to Bromsgrove to 'plead their cause and buy bread'. A song, 'The Nailmakers' Strike', has been handed down to tell the story of the march. The fact that the wagon of coal was presented to the men by another of Halesowen's famous sons, Thomas Attwood, returns us to 'The Leasowes', for his father, Matthias, an ironmaster, purchased the estate in 1806 for his daughter Ann. His third son, Thomas, became a great political reformer. Born in 1783 at Hawne House, Halesowen, he founded the Birmingham Political Union for the Protection of Public Rights in 1830 and was a chief leader in the Chartist movement. He subsequently became an MP and died in 1856 , but it is Birmingham and not his native town that has a statue to his memory.

Whilst still on Mucklow Hill, mention should be made of another old-established firm, Walter Somers', founded in 1866 when the man whose name it bears came from Derbyshire with £100 borrowed from his father and took a lease on an ironworks. A concentration on heavy forging brought prosperity, eventual diversification and in 1963 an amalgamation which made the firm part of a group. Halesowen would not forgive omission of Somers from an account of the town for not only is the name deeply rooted but Frank Somers, one of the founder's two sons, showed a keen interest in local history and published *Halas, Hales, Halesowen* in 1932.

At the foot of Mucklow Hill is the site of a long-gone railway station, for the town has not had a passenger service since 1928, although workmen's trains carried Black Country employees to and from the Austin Motor Works at Longbridge, Birmingham, until the late 1950s. This line played an unwitting part in the development of the first Austin 7 car, although the story really belongs to Old Hill 'up the road' when a lad named Stan Edge got a job in the drawing office at the Austin works. His starting time was nine o'clock (gentleman's hours in the 1920s) but because he had to travel by train to Rubery, the station for the works, he had to catch an early workman's train which caused him to be an hour early. Instead of hanging about, he went in to work, so when Herbert Austin (later Sir), an early bird himself, walked round to see what his draughtsmen were doing, he found Stan Edge hard at work and naturally thought how keen the lad was. As a result, when Herbert Austin decided to build a small car, he chose Stan as his private draughtsman and whisked him away to his home to work with him at an improvised drawing office in the billiard room. This was in 1921, and by Whit Monday 1922 the first car was built and shown to the public – they didn't waste time in those days! The fact that Stan was the only man to work with his boss in the original stages of the design is recognized today by the Austin 7 Clubs' Association.

Apart from this accidental contribution to motoring history, the railway through Halesowen, like the canal before it, played a vital part in getting goods in and out of a town surrounded by hills. Nowadays fast roads have taken over these duties without encroaching on the town centre, and the M5 motorway junction 3 is only a mile distant.

The question as to whether or not Halesowen is on the edge of the coalfield is easily answered, for not only had coal been worked since the thirteenth century but as late as the 1920s there existed the Hawne and Witley collieries on opposite sides of the main Stourbridge Road a little over a mile from the town. Hawne was lost during the 1926 General Strike due to flooding, when the pumps went unmanned (an engine house has been restored and can be seen in Hayseech Road), and Witley closed in 1921 for a similar reason. Coombeswood was another pit, enduring until 1948 and operated under NCB licence after nationalization a year earlier. This brings us to the most industrialized part of Halesowen, for here in a hollow lies Coombeswood Tube Works, built in 1860, eventually part of the once great Stewart & Lloyd organization and now part of the British Steel Corporation, still making tubes but nowhere near the vast enterprise of old.

Having dealt with the most important of Halesowen's collieries and the oldest of its works, we need to return to Hayseech Road for a glimpse of yet another old local industry, evident at a cluster of restored buildings described on a notice as the Gun Barrel Industrial Centre. A three-storey building here was once a farmhouse dating to 1770, whilst the gun-barrel factory still bears the date 1801. Strictly this fascinating little area is in Old Hill but, as a retired postman walking his dog told me, 'We don't know where we are now with so many boundary changes.'

A walk along Hayseech Road over a little bridge across the River Stour, along Hawne Lane and on beside a brook at Bell Vale, a pleasant stretch with mature hedges and plenty of green where industrial scars have healed, brings one to the Stourbridge Road. On the other side a surprise awaits in the shape of Luttley Mill, a building which has somehow survived where so many have vanished, although it has not been in working order this century. The broken wheel is still there, and whilst one hears of intentions to restore it, this has not yet happened. There is a signposted footpath leading off modern Luttley Mill Road but the mill cannot properly be seen without intruding on the residents of the mill house; neither can a plaque on the mill building dated 1823 and marking the old Shropshire/-Worcestershire border. The brook here is a barrier holding back the mass of houses piling up the hillside towards Cradley.

To avoid retracing one's steps along Belle Vale, one can reach Cradley by proceeding west from Luttley Mill up Drew's Holloway and Windmill Hill, where can be seen Ye Olde Lion inn, boldly stating on its façade that it was licensed in the reign of William IV, then down Furlong Lane. 'Cradelie' is mentioned in Domesday as being held by William Fitz Ansculf but it appears to have played little part in history, achieving prominence in the nineteenth-century as a centre of chain-making, a distinction shared with its neighbour, Cradley Heath. The two locations are barely distinguishable, yet each is fiercely guarded by its receptive inhabitants of mature years.

The River Stour is still with us, finding its own level from the Hayseech gun-barrel works and in so doing giving Cradley its oldest link with industry – Cradley Forge, dating to the early seventeenth century and believed, though not proven, for he controlled several forges, to have been the site of Dud Dudley's attempts to smelt iron with coal. This area developed after 1810 into what was to become the vast Corngreaves Iron Company with works and collieries which stripped away the rural aspect and ignored distinctions between the two Cradleys. After various tribulations it closed in 1894, the site becoming semi-derelict and down-at-heel until an influx of new enterprises in the 1970s, but even collectively these modern concerns can never equate with the sprawling works of the last century.

Corngreaves Road is a reminder of the former works, as also is Corngreaves Hall close to the junction of Hawne Lane and Belle Vale. The hall is a relic that perhaps ought not to have survived to have large sums of money spent on it in a time of recession. When I approached through the remains of a stone gateway on an autumn day in 1984, it hardly seemed worth bothering about, a late eighteenth-century building with an early nineteenth-century castellated Gothic frontage and a 'Keep Out. Danger' notice to underline its condition. Once the home of the Attwood family of ironmasters, it has in part been in use as a golf house, the adjacent nine-hole golf course soon to be extended into eighteen. Whether the hall *will* actually be restored as planned is something only the future can determine.

Chainmaking in the Cradleys is said to have been at its most prosperous at the end of the nineteenth century, when each week about a thousand tons of chain were produced: mostly light chain as opposed to massive anchor chain and covering everything from chain for cranes, cart and plough traces, cow-ties and dog chains. A writer visiting the area in 1896 at the request of the Chainmakers' Union, and who admitted to sneaking over back walls of chainworks to get his story, wrote of sheds with five or six women workers, each at an anvil, and a pole running across the room from which dangled chairs for babies so that a mother could rock her child as she worked. One woman said she worked until five o'clock on the day her child was born, her job being to make chain harrows for twelve hours a day to earn 5 shillings a week. A little girl danced on a pair of bellows for 3 pence (3d) a day to supply 'blast' to the forge. Another woman forged dog chains for which, with swivel and ring, she could earn

6 pence (6d.) in a ten-hour day. There was also a female version of the nail fogger. For every hundredweight of chain she received 5s. 4d, for which she paid out 2s. 10d. This contravened the union's agreed twenty-five per cent allowance to the fogger – 'anything over being considered sweating'.

The Chainmakers' and Strikers' Association, as the union was called (a striker in this context being one who wielded a hammer), was formed in 1889 precisely to combat such slavery, and their motto was 'United is Strength.' Clearly it was not very successful in the early years but by the time of the Association's silver jubilee in 1914 it was able to log twelve hundred members and claim that, 'While benefiting ourselves we have also brought advantages to the trade as a whole.' The Association was led by many distinguished figures, closing down in 1977 when no longer needed. The last of the female hand chainmakers, Lucy Woodall (1899-1979), became a minor celebrity in her latter years. She had started in the trade at the age of thirteen and worked a twelve-hour day initially for 4 shillings a week. After a lifetime of work at the anvil, she retired in 1969 but was back at work within a few weeks!

There have been many Ragged Schools in the Black Country but the one which stands out, being well documented and still in existence, is that at Two Gates, Cradley. The first Ragged School was started in Portsmouth in 1767, but this is much later, having been built in 1867 with – so it is said – money raised by the selling of bricks at a penny each. Its survival serves as a reminder of days when, as the chainmaker's plight testifies, 'ragged' was a polite expression of their sad lot.

Judging by the industrial squalor and poverty, it would seem unlikely that Cradley would produce a man destined to give his name to a type-face still used in printing today – Caslon. But when William Caslon was born in 1693 it was a very different Cradley, mainly agricultural except for nailors and various forges along the little river, and in any case it was in eighteenth-century London that he learned type-founding, so successfully that it is said he was responsible for ending Dutch supremacy in the supply of type faces to English printers. He died in 1766, and his name is perpetuated in Halesowen's modern Caslon Hall.

Cradley Heath produced a very different character of note in the present century. Speak of the history of the Staffordshire bull terrier and the name Joe Mallen (1891-1975) will surely be mentioned by enthusiasts of the breed, for he was a co-instigator of the first Staffordshire Bull Terrier Club, formed in 1935 at the Old Cross Guns public house where he was manager. The Old English bulldog weighed about seventy pounds, and it was by crossing with various types of terrier that a dog of just over forty pounds was produced – the Stafford – possessing the tenacity of the bulldog with greater speed and intelligence. Until 1935 it was not recognized by the Kennel Club, and it was due to the efforts of Joe and a few pals that recognition was allowed. However, Joe Mallen was a great character himself, spending fifty-four years in the chain trade working on the 'big 'uns' and retiring with a character reference which read: 'None to surpass, few to equal'. A film, *Joe the Chainsmith*, survives, a copy in the keeping of the Black Country Society as a reminder of the six-foot-tall chainmaker who, in addition to his years of heavy toil and pub management, found time to judge dog shows all over the country.

We have not quite finished with chain, still a viable part of the area's activities although the trend is more towards lifting gear generally – horror of horrors, chain is imported from Spain to its traditional English home! However, the majority of small firms in the Cradleys have won through the recession, and one managing director in particular is forthright in bemoaning the fact that the media are not interested in good news stories.

Mention has been made of a brewery in Dudley trading under the name of a female, and here in Cradley is another woman's firm, the world-famous Eliza Tinsley & Co., manufacturers of chain and holloware for over a hundred years after the death of Eliza. Born Eliza Butler into a nailmaking family, she married a nailmonger named Tinsley and bore him six children. When he died, in 1851, she carried on the business for over twenty years, selling out to a partnership. The fifth generation of one of those partners keeps the firm flourishing today.

Industry apart, the Cradleys have little to show other than churches and chapels of no great distinction. Cradley's parish church of St Peter stands high at the corner of Blue Ball Lane and Mapletree Lane and was erected in 1789 as a Nonconformist chapel before the minister conformed to the Church of England and it was consecrated by the Bishop of Worcester. The building was improved and restored in 1875, and in 1933 further restoration had to be carried out due to mining subsidence. Nonconformists moved around the Black Country, and it is on record that a group came over the dorsal ridge from Darlaston to Cradley Heath where they used a nailworker's shop for worship until founding Grainger's Lane Methodist Church in 1827.

The Cradleys today are a hotch-potch of factories, derelict, over-grown valleys of tangled green, and modern housing bravely trying to impose an up-market image. At the Five Ways, Cradley Heath, the church on the corner has long been a kind of market hall and the long High Street – the main shopping centre – includes a typical (almost mandatory) precinct amid a miscellany of big stores and tiny shops. Attempts continue to be made to upgrade the town and attract shoppers back from the bigger centres of Dudley, Halesowen and Stourbridge. Evidence of this can be seen in the modern railway station and adjacent bus station/car-parks: an attempt to inject a new importance – expresses now stop there – and to encourage commuters to Birmingham to use public transport. Incidentally, one of the few level-crossing gates in the Black Country is to be seen here.

Leaving Five Ways along St Anne's Road and into Dudley Wood Road brings one to the Stadium, home of 'the Heathens', which, as any follower of the sport will know, is a speedway racing club. Formed in 1947 with more enthusiasm than experience, it faded away in 1952, was revived in 1960 and has made an impact on that particular sporting scene. It is perhaps the town's one claim to distinction, and the supporters' battle-cry 'Ommer 'Em Cradley' typifies Black Country disregard for the aspirate.

Old Hill is only three-quarters of a mile from Cradley Heath along the High Street and its continuance Reddall Hill Road, at the end of which is the Cross, merely an offset crossroads and shopping area. Surprisingly, far from being on a hill, Old Hill is at the foot of several inclines, a possible explanation being that it was once referred to as the Old Dell. There is little of outstanding interest until one heads west along Halesowen Road towards the station, past the end of the inappropriately named Beauty Bank and a spread of municipal building to Haden Hill Park, opposite which is the Rose and Crown public house, a modernized version of Stan Edge's home when he worked on the design of the first Austin 7.

Inside the park is the now restored sixteenth-century Haden Hall. Conservationists fought hard and long to save it, and it seemed that hopes of success were doomed when a fire occurred, but saved it is, preserving a link with a family named Haudene (Haden) who were probably awarded the land by the Conqueror for services rendered. This family continued in possession until 1876, whereupon, with the death of Anne Eliza, an eighty-six-year-old spinster, it passed to another branch of the family. The park rolling down the hillside towards Halesowen was landscaped, and in 1922 it became a public park, a delightful 'natural' area still, extending far down into the valley in the direction of the previously mentioned golf course and gun-barrel works.

Next to the old hall, so close that it has led to confusion, is Haden Hill House, built in 1878, when presumably the old hall became untenable. This too has been restored. Close by is a more modern amenity, a ski-slope, and beyond, on the Old Hill side fronting Barrs Road, is the Haden Hill Leisure Centre with swimming bath and gymnasium. Barrs Road takes its name from an offshoot of the Haden family, and later we shall meet the ambitious and some would say fanatical Reverend George Barrs.

Before leaving this area it is interesting on a cultural level to note that such an unlikely place as Old Hill produced a film sponsor as early as 1919. The Reverend Sabine Baring-Gould, a native of Exeter, had writen a novel entitled *Bladys of the Stewponey* – the Stewponey being an inn just outside the Black Country to the west of Stourbridge – and Ben Priest, an Old Hill nut and bolt manufacturer who also owned some local cinemas, gathered a film crew together to make a film of the book as a special attraction for his patrons. A powerful nineteenth-century melodrama, it was shot in and around the local beauty spot of Kinver and duly screened, only to vanish. However, a few frames survived, kept in a tobacco tin for over fifty years, and from these photographic prints have been made for posterity. Benjamin Priest & Sons is still the name of a nut and bolt manufacturer in Old Hill: changes occur but the past is never far away in this area of the Midlands.

Passing mention should be made of Quarry Bank (or 'Bonk' as they say hereabouts), a relatively small 'village' once within the vast parish of Kingswinford. It lies between Brierley Hill and

Cradley and in terms of traditional industry can be linked with the latter for nail- and chain-making, being only a half mile from Mushroom Green chainshop. The main street of run-down shops is very steep, giving a view of typical Black Country sprawl interspersed with housing. Christ Church in the High Street is an impressive mid-nineteenth-century building constructed of local yellow firebrick – as also is the church at Amblecote which we shall visit presently – and has a hammerbeam roof which is probably more impressive since the galleries have been removed.

Nearby, with the main entrance on Thorns Road but best approached down by the church along Park Road, is Stevens Park, presented by local manufacturer and benefactor Ernest Stevens and his wife in 1921. It is the setting for an extensive war memorial within an enclosure dominated by a large bronze figure of Christ on a giant plinth. The absence of graffiti here is commendable.

10

Stourbridge and Lye, Brierley Hill and Kingswinford

The link here is glassmaking, for whilst there were glasshouses in old Dudley town, it is in these localities that it is mostly associated, leading to the term 'Stourbridge glass' so well known today. Lye and that part of Stourbridge known as Amblecote had the right type of clay to prompt the early glassmakers to settle; Kingswinford is where the earliest glassmaking families are first mentioned in the region and where a major glass museum now exists, and Brierley Hill is the home of the oldest of the surviving glassworks. Moreover, between Amblecote and Kingswinford, at Wordsley, is the only remaining glasshouse cone, still in use. Thus we have the industry nicely corralled to return to later.

At the time of Domesday Stourbridge was in the parish of 'Suineforde' (present-day Old Swinford) and held by that same William Fitz Ansculf with whom we are by now familiar. According to Nash, Stourbridge ('Sturbrugge') was first mentioned in the Subsidy Rolls of 1333, and although the town was granted a market in 1482, it may not have been the first. Market day was on a Friday until the market hall, opened in 1827, turned it into an everyday affair. Until modern times the town was in the northern corner of Worcestershire and considered by Black Country folk to be a pleasant market town on the edge of the coalfield with a touch more 'class' than Dudley as well as being an overcoat warmer.

Woollen goods were produced in the seventeenth century, marking a step into industry, and the Gig Mill public house on the corner of South Road and the Broadway serves as a reminder, a gig being a machine by which the nap is raised on cloth. The trade died out and was replaced by extensive coal and fireclay mining (sometimes both being extracted from the same pit) to a degree that put earlier mining activities at Amblecote and Lye firmly in the shade. When the Staffs and Worcs Canal was opened in 1772, followed by the Stourbridge Canal seven years later, the next step was to bring the canal network into the heart of Stourbridge, achieved by constructing a 1¼-mile 'arm'. This was the signal for the start of ironmaking in Stourbridge, and in 1800 Bradley's ironworks were established between the canal and the River Stour. So successful was it that twenty years later it was described as 'the largest complex of any of this part of the country, and perhaps the most so of any in England'.

The Stourbridge Canal Arm remained vital to the town's industrial prosperity even when augmented by the railway, and here one is not discussing long-dead water for it has survived despite attempts at closure. In 1962, when a rally was held and a hundred narrow boats congregated at Stourbridge, a massive clean-up operation was necessary to get rid of mud, rubbish and weeds. It was said that not even a canoe could have got through three weeks before the rally, and it is sadly true that neglected waterways tend to provide receptacles for unwanted household debris. Attempts to retain the Arm eventually succeeded, and in 1984 a bonded warehouse dated 1849 and sited at the terminal point in Canal Street was partly restored and opened to the public, a major event in local canal history, alerting many people to the fact that there is indeed a canal just off the High Street. Extensive towpath walks can be made to Wordsley and down to the junction with the Staffs and Worcs, or towards Dudley looping around Netherton to Warrens Hall Park.

But the ironworks were to give Stourbridge international status earlier than did its celebrated lead crystal glass. By the 1820s James Foster of Bradleys had entered into partnership with an engineer named Rastrick, and they formed a new company just across the river. It is here that in 1829 two historic locomotives were built – *The Agenoria* and *The Stourbridge Lion*. The former has already been mentioned as operating locally for thirty years and is now preserved at the Railway Museum, York. *The Stourbridge Lion*, however, went further afield and has the distinction of having been the first steam locomotive to run on rails in America.

It happened like this. In 1827 the Delaware & Hudson Canal Company of Pennsylvania became interested in the development of the steam-engine for locomotion known to be taking place in England and considered the possibility of buying one to haul coals from its mines near the town of Honesdale. An engineer duly arrived in Britain and ordered an engine from George Stephenson, then busily engaged on building his famous *Rocket*, and, perhaps at his suggestion, found his way to Foster & Rastrick, from whom he ordered three locomotives of the same type as *The Agenoria*. The Stephenson-built *America* actually arrived first in New York, but having studied all four engines the engineer chose *The Stourbridge Lion* as the most promising. Some three miles of track had been laid and crowds assembled for the trials on 8 August 1829. An account reads: 'The crowds continued to cheer in wonder bordering on awe as the iron steed snorted along the ribbons of wood and steel, crossing the Lackawaxen River and disappearing from sight. Many thought it would not return, but after due time with Allen (the engineer) at the controls, and riding backwards, the curious contraption pulled up amidst a great burst of applause ...'

Stourbridge's 'curious contraption' was placed in storage because its total weight of eleven tons including tender was too much for the rails to support. Over the years bits of the locomotive disappeared, and what is left, principally the boiler, two walking beams and a cylinder, is housed in the Hall of Transportation at the Smithsonian Museum, Washington. America has always been willing to acknowledge *The Stourbridge Lion*, and a huge granite boulder suitably inscribed was placed near the spot where the trial took place at the time of the locomotive's centenary celebrations in 1929. Three years later a full-size replica was built, and this is also on view at Honesdale. More recently, on the 150th anniversary in 1979, the Black Country Society produced a limited edition Stourbridge Lion glass goblet bearing an illustration of the engine, and a party of American enthusiasts came to the Black Country for the occasion.

The commemorative goblet leads us back to glass and a suitable point to look in some detail at the industry. All Stourbridge glass today is made outside the original boundary of the old town, the last actually within the former borough being the Heath Glass House, closed in the 1850s and situated close to the one-time council house in Mary Stevens Park. The nearest survivors are at Amblecote, brought into Stourbridge during boundary changes in 1966 and creating confusion because Stourbridge is traditionally in Worcestershire whereas Amblecote was part of South Staffordshire. Thus by acquisition did Stourbridge regain a stake in its own industry, for here at Amblecote is the firm of Webb Corbett, dating under various names to the early nineteenth century and occupying part of a former Huguenot factory when they commenced production of English lead crystal in 1879. A fire in 1913 brought the company to its present site. Also at Amblecote is the Dennis Hall Glassworks of Thomas Webb & Sons, a family which entered the business in 1829 at Wordsley, moving to the present site in the 1850s. Dennis Hall, a Georgian mansion, is now part of the factory.

One cannot cover even the handful of glass-manufacturers that remain – indeed, one or two newcomers have entered the trade in a small way – but mention must be made of the Red House Glassworks at Wordsley if for no other reason that it has the last surviving glasshouse cone, dating to about 1790, restored in the 1980s and now a working museum open to visitors. This is the home of Stuart Crystal, the Stuart family having been connected with the works since 1827. The trade name Stuart Crystal appeared in 1927, as did the practice of etching the name Stuart on each piece of glass produced.

To conclude even this brief survey of glass-manufacture, so important to the area, one needs to nip smartly up to Brierley Hill to the oldest surviving works, Stevens & Williams, who trade as Royal Brierley Crystal and date their origins as coinciding with the passing of the 1776 Act to build the Stourbridge Canal. Still in the Williams family, present-day production falls roughly into two categories: stem ware and gift ware. Each of these leading firms has sales shops on the premises, and coach parties come from considerable distances to make guided tours of the works. The impact of the Stourbridge glass industry is felt right

Brick-built railway viaduct at Stourbridge. It has ten arches and was built in 1881 to replace a wooden structure

The last remaining glasshouse cone in the Black Country – Stuart
Crystal, Wordsley

ft: The picturesque tower of the King Edward VI College, Stourbridge

Holy Trinity Church at Wordsley. Note the external steel bands reinforcing the tower

St Mark's Church, Pensnett, saved from the effects of mines and ironworks

A 'feature' pit head gear and engine house at the entrance to Pensnett
Trading Estate

The Vine (better known as the Bull and Bladder), Delph, Brierley Hill,
with its Shakespearean quotation on the façade

The Glynne Arms, commonly known as the Crooked House, Himley

The 1937 Coronation Gardens at the top of Owen Street, Tipton.
Modern housing backs on to the canal

A touch of the rural – Portway Farmhouse on Portway Hill, Rowley
Regis, as it sweeps towards Oldbury

Remains of a windmill at Ruiton, Gornal

across the Black Country so that, when someone is leaving a job, and for umpteen kinds of anniversary, the first thought is to 'get some cut glass' generally a rose bowl or vase. As a result many households have built up collections, often handed down, and a true story of two women talking following a wartime air raid underlines the value attached to such items.

'They were close last night, weren't they, Vi?'

'Arr! If 'e'd 'ad it [the bomb] in 'is other 'ond we'd 'ave 'ad it.'

'Pity about that couple though.'

'Arr! An' all that cut glass gone.'

Had it been a joke, it would have been typical of the cruel streak in Black Country humour. It wasn't! It was a spontaneous choice in priorities.

Should glassworks' visitors wish to see modern Stourbridge, they first have to get into the town, for it is contained within a tight oval by a ring road about a mile round and having the appearance of a racetrack. The town is virtually isolated by this much-criticized road, the disadvantages aggravated by the smallness of the central area and increased pedestrianization. True, bus and train stations are just across the ring road, but they are on higher ground, a factor which, combined with an underpass that is anything but direct, effectively prevents the aged infirm from entering the shopping area under their own steam.

The centre point, as in so many towns, is a clock, but this is taller than most and cast into the base are the words 'This column was constructed at the Stourbridge ironworks 1857', a reminder of the town's industrial heyday. The clock stands outside the former market hall, whose façade has been preserved during extensive development which includes the Crown Centre complex. The shops proved difficult to let, and for long it was branded a white elephant as people demanded to know what the town wanted with more shops when old-established High Street stores were closing? However, the complex includes the nineteenth-century town hall which has been cleaned up and renovated, and this, plus a modern library and rooms for meetings and dances, has given the town a cultural boost. Building trends in the 1980s have veered away from concrete, and a rash of dark-red brick has appeared throughout the region, of which the Crown Centre is an example. Looking at its back-end bulk from Enville Street to the west, it looks like the bastion of a fortress in modern dress so that strangers might be forgiven for thinking that Stourbridge has become a walled town.

Not that there is much of historic interest in this central area other than the former King Edward VI grammar school, now a sixth-form college, the Church of St Thomas, the Talbot Hotel and, at the bottom of Lower High Street, a Presbyterian chapel opened in 1788 and claimed to be one of the few to retain so exactly the characteristics of an eighteenth-century meeting house. The school, said to have received its charter in 1552, has had a varied career, the buildings today being nineteenth-century with early twentieth-century additions (Pevsner describes the tower as picturesque), whilst St Thomas' Church, which was started in 1728 but not consecrated until 1866, stands in Market Street opposite the Ryemarket shopping precinct. The Talbot Hotel in the High Street is the town's most ancient hostelry, said to be five hundred years old and, according to one local historian, 'the one place in Stourbridge everybody knew and Stourbridge was judged by it'.

Beyond the confines of the ring road but fronting it is the Roman Catholic Church of Our Lady and All Saints opened in 1864. The 130-foot spire was added in 1889, and extensive restoration was carried out in the 1960s. Another home of religion but of a very different order, visible from the ring road just before leaving it for Amblecote, is the seventeenth-century Quaker meeting house actually in Scott Street. In 1984 the members had the bright idea of holding an open day to acquaint the public with their form of worship. Fascinating documents were on display showing that Quakers had gathered in Stourbridge in the 1650s. Quakers were imprisoned and their goods seized for refusing to pay church rates or tithes, and in 1674 one Sarah Reynolds, a widow of Stourbridge with five small children, was fined for refusing to pay a rate of 9 pence (9d).

Stourbridge has many industries, and as one leaves the ring road towards Amblecote a factory roof bearing the name Attwood is clearly visible. This is the nineteenth-century firm of Jones & Attwood, an early manufacturer of penny-farthing bicycles and in modern times known throughout the world for sewage-treatment plant and other products. As a leader manufacturer, this company like a host of others would have looked forward to the arrival of the railway when in 1852 the Oxford, Worcester & Wolverhampton was built, the station being just over a half mile from the town at what became known as the Junction, where the line joined one to Birmingham. A goods line was constructed in 1861 to link the town with the Junction, and this extended to Amblecote, where a depot was constructed. The busy goods depot and engine sheds that subsequently developed there, along with the adjacent canal arm, created a major traffic centre – yet another surprise to those who regard Stourbridge as being semi-rural. Now all has gone, for British Rail closed the goods yards and sheds in 1965. It is interesting to note, however, that the Penfields housing estate now occupying part of the goods depot site has street names commemorating famous locomotive-builders such as Gooch and Churchward. The line from the town's Foster Street Station to the Junction remains open despite periodic rumours of closure, and since the town station was modernized as recently as 1979, it may be that one will still be able to travel for some years to come on what must be British Rail's shortest line.

One of Stourbridge's best-known structures is the viaduct which carries the railway over the valley of the River Stour at Stambermill on the road to Lye. Originally a wooden structure, it was replaced in 1881 by the present impressive fifty-eight-foot-high brick viaduct of ten arches having a span of $46\frac{1}{2}$ feet.

Close to Stourbridge Junction is a public house with the unusual name 'The Labour in Vain', its sign no longer swinging bravely over the pavement but pinned less conspicuously to the wall. It shows two women trying to scrub a black boy! At this point one is at Old Swinford and close to it the Church of St Mary, the mother church of Stourbridge, set at the end of a quiet backwater that could be the focal point of some rural community, as once it surely was. There has been a church here since the thirteenth century, but apart from the fourteenth-century tower, the present building is nineteenth-century, restored as recently as 1938. Walk down Glasshouse Hill and Heath Lane, and Mary Stevens Park is reached. This is the town's premier park and owes its existence to that same Ernest Stevens who gave the park at Quarry Bank. It was donated in memory of his wife in 1929, and the main entrance gates are still there with their ornamental transom and a lantern on each of the four massive pillars. Inside the park a broad avenue leads to the Heath Pool past a war memorial unveiled by the Earl of Coventry in 1923.

Amblecote was itself in Domesday and like Old Swinford more identifiable than was the 'bridge over the Stour' eventually to become Stourbridge. Amblecote's parish church was St Mary's at Old Swinford, and not until 1824 did it have its own church of the Holy Trinity, like Quarry Bank's church utilizing firebricks in its construction. Considering the area abounded in fire clay, why not make use of it? By 1850 the Stourbridge area alone was producing some fourteen million firebricks a year from six principle mines – fireclay was mined rather than dug – and we are told that in 1864 there were at least 117 firms across the Black Country engaged in brickmaking. Thousands of 'Coronation Streets' throughout the country must have been built of Black Country brick. It was a female-intensive industry, and young girls bore heavy lumps of wet clay to benches for older women to work into shape, not just for bricks but for furnace linings, glasshouse pots, paving tiles and so forth. Physical stamina was more important than skill, and as old photographs illustrate, local women were well suited, although, as a strike in 1913 highlighted, they were paid less even than the women chainmakers who believed that they held the doubtful honour of being at the bottom of the wage table.

Opposite Amblecote church in Vicarage Road is the Corbett Hospital, demoted in 1984 in deference to the newly-opened Russells Hall Hospital at Dudley to which the casualty department was moved. One reads today that salt is a potential health hazard, yet that was the commodity to which the Corbett Hospital owes it origin. John Corbett was born at Brierley Hill in 1817, the son of a canal boat operator. He was in his late twenties when he bought a derelict brine works at Stoke Prior near Bromsgrove and built it up to be the most successful in the country, earning the title of 'Salt King'. He was a great philanthropist, and one of his good deeds was to offer his Georgian mansion, 'The Hill', Amblecote, for conversion into a hospital. His offer was accepted and the hospital was opened in 1893. By the time of his death, in 1901, the hospital was well established and the August Bank holiday Corbett Hospital fêtes, destined to be a major event in the local calendar, had already seized public imagination with balloon ascents and all the fun of the fair.

Opposite Vicarage Road is the athletic ground where the Stourbridge football and cricket clubs battle out their home matches, whilst further down the main road is the Fish Inn, a public house that has given its name to the crossroads here. It is from 'The Fish' that the Kinver tram departed, its outstanding feature being that for some 1¼ miles of its journey at the Kinver end it ran across fields, crossing the meandering River Stour at several points on wooden bridges and at one place skirting the Staffs and Worcs Canal. There can have been no tram ride of greater scenic beauty anywhere than that enjoyed by passengers using the line between its opening in 1901 and closure in 1930. Black Country folk made for Kinver in droves, and traffic reached its peak on Whit Monday 1905 when no fewer than 16,699 passengers were carried. The toastrack trams continued to run late into the night until every passenger had been returned to the conurbation. Moreover, the line linked at Amblecote with the main Black Country tramway system, and in those days there was scarcely a locality – or a factory of note – that was not served by a tram route. Traces of the cross-country Kinver tram can still be seen, and it is a great pity that the line could not have been preserved for posterity. What an attraction it would be today!

Lye is an appendage of Stourbridge far different in heritage and character, definitively known as 'the Lye', possibly because it was unlike anywhere else – the last place God ever made, according to some commentators – and indeed much of it was 'waste' even in the late nineteenth century, as evidenced in some locally written verses issued in 1878 under the title 'The Lye Waste Soup Shop'. It is worth quoting in part, for not only does it underline the poverty of the time but it indicates how the inhabitants were known by nicknames.

Three times in a week this soup is to be sold,
To lame, or to lazy, or to old,
To tailors and nailors and chainmakers too,
To colliers and spademakers, many and few.

This soup being ready, the sale did begin.
Moll Dondy was first, so she quickly got in.

But in a few minutes there was such a crowd,
Such pushing and shoving, some cried out loud.

As Wockum was pushing to get to the door,
With Pongey and Tacker, and two or three more,
Old Tuckey and Figup, they rushed with such might
As made Wockum to grumble and challenge to fight.

So it goes on through many verses, with reference to Nell
Gourge, Latchet and Tinkey and Wobber and Crabb, Crackback
and Mow and Fire-lock and Shaggsby. How they came by such
strange names we shall never know.

As has been shown, the River Stour played a vital part in the
development of the western side of the Black Country, and here
at Lye the story is the same, for Lye Forge (now commemorated
by the Old Forge Trading Estate) dates to at least 1699, when a
water-driven helve hammer was set up on the river bank by one
James Folkes, whose descendants have continued in engineering
and building development to the present day as part of a large
organisation. When John Folkes died, in 1844, he was succeeded
by his son Constantine, who gained for himself the title 'King of
Lye' and is said to have been deeply religious, making himself
unpopular through his attempts to secure a proper observance of
the Lord's Day. Religion came late to Lye, and from 1790 to 1792
a certain Reverend James Scott conducted services in licensed
dwelling houses on Lye Waste. A Unitarian chapel was opened in
1806, the first place of worship ever built at Lye. Another chapel
was opened in 1861 on land adjoining, and these 'two buildings in
one' complete with clocktower still exist in the High Street.
Christ Church followed in 1813 and a Methodist church
appeared in 1837, the latter renovated and reopened in its
centenary year.

Lye's main shopping centre is along the main road from
Stourbridge to Halesowen and Birmingham, and therein lies one
of its chief problems – congestion. Traders have fought for years
to prevent car-parking from being banned in the narrow main
street, many of its shops are empty, and its future as a viable
community is in doubt. The centre point, Lye Cross, is the
birthplace of one of Britain's most celebrated actors, Cedric
Hardwicke, although the house in which he was born on 10
February 1893 has long since been demolished. Like Brett

Young's, Cedric's father was a doctor, and the actor once related how he had been taken on a tour of the district where he saw 'slums and backyards which always seemed without sunlight, families of more than a dozen living in one room, ragged children slaving next to parents in grim chainshops'. Knighted in 1934, he returned to Lye in the following year to open a new library, making a speech in which he said generously, if tongue in cheek, that he owed a great deal more to Lye than possibly Lye people could owe to him. He died in New York in 1964.

Between Stourbridge and the Delph at Brierley Hill – that pre-industrial hill of briars – is a vast housing complex built on an open-cast coal-mining site which in the early 1970s created an artificial mountain of spoil that looked as if it was there to stay. A large number of pit shafts were discovered and in-filled during which several mining tools were found in the workings where they had lain for perhaps a hundred years. Here was the area's most prolific clay/coal-producing spot with a preponderance of the former, and much of the ground now tends to be low-lying especially that residential part known as Withymoor Village. Withymoor is an old-established name, for a certain scythe blade and spademaker issued his Withymoor penny token in 1813-14. Said to be one of the most informative tokens ever produced, it gives on the obverse side a complete picture of a powered forge shop of the day, the reverse depicting the products manufactured.

At the Delph Road end of Withymoor Village stands the Vine public house, known locally as 'the Bull and Bladder' and a magnet for the beer-drinking fraternity on account of its home-brewed ale. It also has the rare distinction of having a line from Shakespeare blazoned large over the façade – 'Blessing of your heart you brew good ale.'

Nearby, off Delph Road, are the Nine Locks of the Dudley No. 1 Canal, notable in typical Black Country fashion because there are only eight, due to rebuilding in 1857. The earlier figure has to some extent been perpetuated by the Nine Locks Colliery, otherwise known as the Earl of Dudley's No. 29 pit, where a disaster in 1869 set in motion one of the most remarkable rescue operations in the history of the region. In short, the pit became flooded with thirteen men missing. It was hoped that, as the seam of coal moved upward, the spot where they were known to be working would be dry, and frantic attempts were made to pump out sufficient water to lower the level sufficiently to attempt rescue. In fact, the men below were unaware that they were trapped until they finished their stint and found the way blocked by floodwater. After some 130 hours spent mostly in the dark, drinking floodwater, eating their tallow candles and chewing coal, the water level lowered and rescue was achieved by floating to the trapped men on a raft. All but one, who had lost his reason, torn off his clothes and disappeared into the workings, was saved. Like all Black Country pits, No. 29 has long since gone, but the Nine Locks rescue is remembered.

Brierley Hill town straggles the main Dudley-Stourbridge road, and its traders have suffered from being in-betweens, for many folk prefer to shop at one or other of the larger towns. An attempt to rectify the situation is the Moor Centre, completed in 1985, a complex of shops, offices and entertainment. This is partly on the site of the once famous Marsh & Baxter works, and it is sad that a firm which started with the purchase of a small pork butcher's shop in Brierley Hill High Street in 1867 and grew into the biggest sausage- and pie-making concern of its kind has had to go. Modern advertising executives may think they invented the genre, but in the early 1900s Marsh & Baxter producing a poster which surely ranks as a classic: it showed a pig hauling a flat cart on which rested a pack of sausages and the caption read: 'Drawing its own conclusion.'

Brierley Hill's saddest blow in modern times is the loss of the giant Round Oak Steelworks, whose history hones right in on the earls of Dudley and their industrial pre-eminence. Level Street, until the 1970s one of the most unlevel streets likely to be encountered anywhere, links High Street with Pedmore Road, and this is where it all began, following the coming of the canal in 1779. For the first time the mining industry hereabout was able to embark on manufacturing free of the constrictions of road transport, and in 1784 a piece of land was leased from Lord Dudley for the building of blast furnaces. Four years later Benjamin Gibbons was the tenant, and it was he who created rolling mills and started what was to be almost two hundred years of iron- and steel-making. In 1800 Gibbons erected more furnaces on the opposite (northern) side of Level Street, but by 1843 he had moved to a new site at Pensnett, whereupon the

Dudley estate took over these latter furnaces adjacent to which in 1857 the Round Oak works came into being, adding the manufacture of wrought iron to the other activities of the then William, 11th Baron Dudley (later Earl of Dudley). The advent of the Bessemer steel process led to steelmaking in 1894, and Round Oak became all-powerful and synonymous with success until steel nationalization in 1951 finally broke the company's link with the Dudley family.

At its peak Round Oak employed some 3,500 people who along with their families continued to the end, as they had always done, to refer to the plant as 'the Earl's'. Anyone who could boast a job at 'the Earl's' was all right thank you, and the most incredible part of the whole Round Oak story is that massive investment – probably around £20 million – was made in the decade before closure in the early 1980s.

A link between Brierley Hill and Canada is evidenced today by a thoroughfare called Nanaimo – the name being that of a city on Vancouver Island, British Columbia. To discover why there should be a Nanaimo Way in Brierley Hill and a Brierley Hill Road in Nanaimo, one needs to go back to 1854, when the Hudson Bay Company decided to recruit skilled miners from Britain. They appointed a Shropshire man as manager and asked him to engage twenty colliers. He duly signed up suitable men who together with their wives and children sailed on 3 June 1854. The Brierley Hill party numbered eighty-three, and they suffered a terrible voyage during which one man, one woman and four infants died. A century after their departure the Nanaimo section of the British Columbia Historical Society wrote to Brierley Hill council to say that they intended to mark the centenary by re-enacting the landing in the costume of the period, and subsequently the vice-president of that Society visited the Black Country town, starting a chain of events which resulted in Brierley Hill school projects concerning this nineteenth-century migration of local people.

Much of Brierley Hill is in a state of long-term development including the Round Oak Steelworks site which is part of an Enterprise Zone designed to attract new industry, so there is little of historic interest to delay the visitor apart perhaps from the parish church of St Michael which stands at the highest point of the parish. Built of brick in 1765 and known for many years as a chapel, this outwardly plain building has been much altered, the west tower being largely rebuilt in 1900. The interior is said to be rather splendid, the chancel being in the form of a modified apse and separated from the nave by a semi-circular arch on Ionic columns.

Approaching Kingswinford from Amblecote, one passes the Red House Glassworks and through the village of Wordsley where a nineteenth-century church graces the skyline. This is Holy Trinity, consecrated in 1831 and from then on becoming the parish church of Kingswinford until 1846. It was extensively restored in 1977 and 1981, the tower being reinforced by external steel bands. Further along the main road is Wordsley Hospital, an old-fashioned building which originated as a workhouse with all the grimness that implies but today renowned among other things for its plastic surgery unit.

Kingswinford is soon reached, and since the earliest Huguenot glassmakers settled here, it is somehow fitting that in Barnett Lane is the Broadfield House Glass Museum displaying a selection of the region's historic glass with as much again in store, enabling exhibits to be changed. The museum was opened in 1980 despite intense opposition to housing the collection in this former old people's home built in 1822. The collection was started before the Second World War at Brierley Hill, and it was thought that Broadfield House was remote and unknown. In fact it is well signposted, has free car-parking and attracts visitors from all over the world. The building has rooms devoted to the glassblower's craft and to specific local firms, showing a wealth of coloured glass and crystal. Exhibits include Roman, German, French, Scandinavian and American pieces, and there is much contemporary work.

Kingswinford is generally regarded as a residential dormitory village but its oldest part heading toward Dudley is industrial. It is now relatively small although the original parish was over seven thousand acres and included Brierley Hill. The centre point is the Cross, where there is a public house of that name and a modern shopping precinct where a small open market is held, but the most interesting spot is an area designated 'the Village', where there is a green and a secluded avenue leading to St Mary's Church. Basically twelfth-century – the first vicar listed on the role of incumbents being in 1186 – the tower is part

Norman, restored in the seventeenth century, and set in the wall above the vestry door is a Norman tympanum depicting the slaying of the dragon by St Michael (not St George). The building was enlarged in the eighteenth century but closed between 1831 and 1846 when it appeared to be in danger from mining subsidence – which is why the church at Wordsley became the parish church during that period.

On an outside wall of the church is a memorial tablet to one John Horton, an able seaman of HMS *Hood* who 'in a gallant attempt to save others was himself drowned. Nov. 25, 1923'. No: not as one might suppose at sea, but in an ice-covered pool whilst saving the lives of two boys.

In the churchyard stands a stone pillar believed to be the shaft of a medieval preaching cross, from whose base sentences passed at the Old Court House were publicly announced. This building, where the Court Leet was held and parish business transacted, stands on the opposite side of the main road and is now an inn. The Village boasts a number of well-preserved Georgian houses, whilst modern housing flanks the approach to the church.

Kingswinford lost its major historic secular building, sixteenth-century Bradley Hall, in 1924, not through conventional demolition but because it was taken down carefully and transferred to Stratford-upon-Avon where it was re-erected to add to the tally of Tudor residences in Shakespeare's town. Modern Bradley Hall, a home for the aged, is on a different site. Nearby is Summerhill Court, an eighteenth-century mansion and now a hotel. It was once the home of ironmasters, and it was from here on Whit Monday 1909 that Joseph H. Smith set out in his dogcart to his works at Brierley Hill when he was in collision with a governess cart and killed. His firm, Hill & Smith, founded in 1824, still exists on its original site at the end of Canal Street, Brierley Hill – a puddingbag street (cul-de-sac) to Black Country folk.

11

Sedgley, Coseley and the Gornals

Sedgley is an ancient parish mentioned in the Charter of Ethelred in A.D. 985 as 'Seagges Leage', at which time it was far more extensive than it is today, reaching to Coseley and Woodsetton to the east and to Cotwall End, Gospel End and Lower Gornal to the west. The main street forms part of the Wolverhampton-Dudley highway along the dividing ridge of the Black Country. In fact, it is near the end of this high ground for the road soon dips sharply towards Wolverhampton as it skirts Beacon Hill, which is over seven hundred feet above sea-level. The hill is accessible for walking and offers splendid views of enormous contrast: to the west the rural countryside of Worcestershire and Shropshire stretching away to Wales, and to the east the industrial sprawl across the Tame Valley to Barr Beacon and the outline of Cannock Chase.

Atop the hill dwarfed by miscellaneous items of steelwork is a signal tower constructed in stone and built during the last century by Lord Wrottesley to serve as an astrological observatory. If the Black Country was anywhere near as black as nineteenth-century writers maintained, it is difficult to believe that it served its purpose. One such writer dismissed Sedgley as 'uninteresting', but in modern times it has developed as 'a nice place in which to live', having a clean look about it and slightly up-market in parts. Although like Brierley Hill it is midway between large towns, its shops tend to fare better, possibly because of the spread of private housing down both sides of the ridge.

The focal point is the Bull Ring beside which is the Red Lion inn, an ancient hostelry and halt for through coaches. Conservationists maintain that the church and three inns, the Red Lion, the Swan and the Court House (both in Gospel End Street) hold together the old village layout. Where Sedgley does score historically is in its Roman Catholic church of St Chad and All Saints in Catholic Lane, erected in 1823, an early and bold move by the Catholic community since they were not officially granted freedom of worship until 1829. Its existence is due to the fact that there had been a Roman Catholic college at Sedgley Park since 1763, occupying the Park Hall. There is still a Park Hall, now a hotel and actually just inside Wolverhampton.

Closer to the Bull Ring in Vicar Street is the parish church of All Saints, rebuilt and reopened in 1829 at the expense of the Earl of Dudley. It did not require fresh consecration as part of the fourteenth-century tower of the earlier church remained. Parish registers date to 1558.

There will be considerable dodging up and down the ridge in this chapter, so first let us go down Bush Bank as far as Gospel End to the site of Baggeridge Colliery, the last pit of any consequence in the Black Country. The site has been converted into a country park, opened in 1983 by Princess Anne. It is a remarkable transformation, the contrast being apparent should one venture along an adjacent roadway signposted Baggeridge Brickworks, for this concern still flourishes, pinpointed by one of the few remaining tall chimneys to survive out of the hundreds that once belched smoke and soot over the region. This area is on the fringe of open country rich in outdoor amenity, and at the corner of Catholic Lane and Cotwall End Road is Cotwall End Nature Reserve, listed as an area of specialized interest, the valley providing rich and varied natural fauna and flora. The reserve incorporates freshwater pools, a walled garden, an aviary and a specially constructed lair with a viewing window through which one can observe a red fox, and there are all kinds of animals and wildfowl. Admission is free and it is a popular all-year-round venue.

Coseley is a large area embracing such localities as Hurst Hill, Woodsetton and Deepfields, a part of it now in Wolverhampton, a bit nibbling into Bilston and other parts nudging Tipton and Dudley, all lying on the eastern slopes of the ridge. The old village of Coseley has virtually ceased to exist in a form that older people would recognize, and there is considerable dereliction. Probably the most important event of the present century occurred in the late 1920s when an arterial road constructed between Birmingham and Wolverhampton cut through and opened it up as never before. This road of about ten miles was the first major highway in the Black Country to be purpose-built for the age of the internal combustion engine, having a forty-foot carriageway considered exceptional for those days. Proposed initially as a means of relieving local unemployment, it entailed considerable construction problems due to the nature of the terrain, 'formerly used for the purpose of various industrial undertakings such as mining, quarrying and ironworks'. It was anticipated that it would attract industry to the area through which it passed, and so it proved, leading to what was known as ribbon development.

It is said that Coseley and the Gornals had as many chapels and churches as public houses, and whilst it may sound the right order of priority, it is staggering when one considers the vast number of pubs that used to flourish. Nailors and colliers (there were over fifty pits in Coseley alone in the 1830s) lived torn between a need for drink to alleviate their miseries and for redemption through worship. The first meeting house in Coseley was built in 1717, although the list of ministers goes back to the 1660s, and later the rather sinisterly named Darkhouse Chapel was inserting considerable influence with break-away groups carrying their message elsewhere – their incursion into Lye has been noted. The Baptists at Coseley had originally worshipped at a house in the village, converts being baptized in the canal. An off-shoot of this chapel was opened by the Providence Baptists in 1809. Although the ramifications of the various denominational groups is too complex to be attempted here, mention must be made of Sodom. No, this is not an expletive but the genuine name bestowed on a small part of Coseley. Whilst it undoubtedly originated through the wickedness of its inhabitants, it became sufficiently acceptable as actually to appear on the deeds of a certain house of worship. Truly one never knows what inconsistency the Black Country is capable of producing!

Christ Church, Coseley, is an early nineteenth-century building in Church Road separated from the village by the main

electrified railway which fortuitously still provides the area with
a station – Deepfields, whilst on the Sedgley side of the
Birmingham-Wolverhampton 'New' Road is St Mary's, built
some forty years later than Christ Church but which unlike the
latter has no tower. Neither church is of particular interest
although Pevsner credits Christ Church with a 'nice east chapel'.

The furnaces long associated with Deepfields and thereabouts
have long since gone, and the only historical industrial concern of
consequence to survive is one whose name is displayed on electric
cookers and gas fires in every High Street – Cannon. Cannon
Industries date to 1826, when Edward and Stephen Sheldon set
up a small foundry to make 'pots and pans', developing into a
major producer of domestic holloware as well as of those giant
'Kaffir' cooking pots which one associates with Robinson Crusoe
pantomimes. The company began to make gas stoves in 1894,
and in 1905 the first Cannon radiant type gas fires were made,
beginning as a sideline and destined to make worldwide impact.
In 1959 Cannon introduced a new word into the English language
– GasMiser – a trade name that has become synonymous with
fuel economy. The old 1826 building was unhappily gutted by
fire as recently as 1980 but the company continue to be
forerunners in their field.

Now to the Gornals: Upper Gornal on the main Dudley-
Wolverhampton Road along the ridge, Lower Gornal to the west
and Gornal Wood adjacent. Gornal folk are the traditional butt
of Black Country jokes, the home of those mythical characters
Aynuk and Ayli, whose stupidity is legion:

'We're yo' gooin' this mornin'?'

'Ter waerk. We're dun yer think?'

'But yo'm on the road home.'

'Oh arr! Soo I am. I turned me back ter the wind ter light me
pipe an' forgot ter turn round again.'

The story of putting the pig on the wall to watch the band go
by is a bit of Gornalese that prompted one contemporary Gornal
man to have a rubber stamp made of a pig-on-the-wall drawing
to put on his correspondence. No one is offended; after all it
happened in the last century. Or did it? In reality Gornal folk are
shrewd, proud of their heritage and apt to be mistrustful of
anyone 'from off', as they say of newcomers. At the same time
they have 'hearts of gold' and are 'the salt of the earth', and it is

no reflection on these old sayings that the words 'gold' and 'salt' both have special significance here.

Although most local men were miners – they will tell you that Gornal was built on coal – some men as well as women used to travel round the Black Country selling salt from carts. The salt was in large blocks, and the cry would be 'Any sort terday?', demand being considerable in the days when it was used to preserve meat and certain vegetables: for example, runner beans would be preserved by alternating layers of beans and salt. Not to be confused with Gornal salt (in reality from Droitwich) was Gornal sand, quarried locally. This was a very fine sand, having been crushed by a huge stone wheel pulled round and round by horses. Again, this was hawked round the region: 'A ha'penny a bucket an' some in yer 'ond.' This sand was used for scouring and to sprinkle on tiled floors so that when swept up the dirt went with it. Donkeys used to pull the carts, and Gornal became noted far and wide for these animals, cheaply kept since pasture was plentiful. Now that tourism has spread into the Black Country, one can almost imagine a picturesque 'Gornal Hilton' where guests are drawn between floors on ramps by means of donkey carts. Here, anything can happen!

So much for the 'salt' tag, now what about the 'gold'? Well, Gornal folk of old are said to have been distrustful of banks and hung on to their sovereigns, hiding them perhaps behind a loose brick in the chimney. Many jokes have arisen from this assumption, but shortly after the war a young man carrying a biscuit tin walked into a Dudley post office followed reluctantly by an older man. 'I've just persuaded my Dad to dig this up,' the younger man told the clerk. The tin contained bundles of notes mildewed and stuck together, amounting to £1,000, a lot of money in those days. After they had been separated and counted, the post office counter had to be disinfected. A true story!

Within the Gornals the people of that inner locality known as Ruiton were considered more Gornal than Gornal, yet to the uninitiated Ruiton is just the name of a street at the end of which are the remains of a windmill erected in the 1820s to grind corn. It ceased operation in 1871 and stands today without sails or machinery. Serious restoration proposals have so far failed for lack of funds. It is not true that there used to be two windmills but one was taken down because there wasn't enough wind for both!

Religion locally is mainly Noncomformist: a small chapel built in Summit Place in 1805 is thought to be the first Wesleyan Methodist place of worship in Lower Gornal and, when some of its members disagreed in 1836, the Zoar Methodist Chapel, Gornal Wood, was formed. Ruiton Congregational chapel was built in Lower Gornal in 1830, a Wesleyan chapel opened in Upper Gornal two years later, and two cottages used for worship by another group led in 1878 to the building of a church now known as Mount Zion. As for the established Church, St Peter's, Upper Gornal, was opened in 1842 as a chapel of ease to All Saints, Sedgley, and St James', Lower Cornal, consecrated in 1823, was enlarged several times during the last century. Religion in its various forms was and probably still is taken more seriously in the Gornals than in most other localities. Today the Sunday School anniversary continues as a highlight of the year, particularly among chapel folk, who take great pride in seeing their children sing on the platform.

Pigeon-flying has long been a favourite pastime for Black Country folk, and in the Gornals, as elsewhere, it continues to flourish. Many a childhood game has been suspended whilst patient men coaxed their pigeons down from the chimneypots into the pens with tempting handfuls of corn after they had been let out for a fly round. The top end of the pigeon-fancier's world involves racing, and clubs organize transport of birds to the countryside, the coast and even abroad, the return of the birds anxiously awaited. 'If my blighters don't come back, I'll kill 'em,' a despairing fancier might exclaim as competitors' birds home in. The fanaticism of some pigeon-flyers is reflected in the following tale in which a dying collier asked of a visiting parson:

'Shall we have wings in that next world yo' talk about?'

Assured of the scriptural view that angels did indeed have wings, the collier said:

'Well, parson. If yo' have wings and I have wings, when yo' come up I'll fly yer for a quid.'

What of the Gornals today? Upper Gornal has a small shopping centre, its church and very little else; Lower Gornal is more interesting because it retains a village appearance with a shopping centre – even banks now to entice folk to disregard the

chimney and back garden as a depository for savings – whilst
Gornal Wood, little changed, verges onto the road from Dudley
to Himley. Modern housing estates have been built on former
mining areas such as the Straits; the Ellowes Comprehensive
School is a reminder that here was Ellowes Hall, demolished in
1964, the home of a succession of influential ironmasters for some
140 years, and there are probably more people 'from off' living in
the Gornals than there are natives.

Even so, the older family names perpetuate, and one has only
to talk to the 'old uns' to find that the traditional Gornal
character is still very much alive. Tradition dies hard: there is a
thriving Miners' Welfare Club although there hasn't been a pit
to mine since the late 1960s!

Just down the road from Gornal Wood is one of the region's
main attractions – the Crooked House, real name 'the Glynne
Arms', strictly just in Himley but sufficiently Gornalized to
warrant inclusion here. Signposted opposite a converted
tollhouse and approached along a dirt road, the Glynne Arms is
the one pub where one can feel intoxicated even before entering.
Everything about the building is crooked. It tilts at its south end,
with doors, windows and sills set at crazy angles, and it is
difficult to walk steadily through the doorway, for one's figure
appears to lean. The clock on the wall, perpendicular as the
pendulum shows, appears to hang sideways, as do the flex and
fittings of the ceiling lights. Marbles placed on the 'lower' end of
a table apparently roll up hill, providing a constant source of
amusement. The Crooked House has been an attraction for
generations of Black Country folk who before the age of the
motor car travelled by 'shank's pony' (on foot) and gave the
building their own distinctive name of 'the Siden House'.

Apart from its peculiar stance, the inn has historic
associations with the gentry in that it is named after the Glynne
family who built it on their estate, their manor being the nearby
Oak House Farm, demolished before the day of preservation
orders. In 1839 Sir Stephen Glynne, the 9th and last baronet in
the line, became brother-in-law to William Ewart Gladstone, the
great Prime Minister to be, through the latter's marriage to his
sister Catherine. Glynne was persuaded to exploit the coal,
ironstone and clay deposits on his estate, and the Oak Farm
Company was formed, soon to overreach itself and fall into

difficulties. Gladstone came to the rescue and the works prospered for a time but by 1875 everything had been sold and what had been described as the most disastrous excursion into the world of iron-production came to an end. No trace of this once extensive complex remains, but the fields and woodland still bear the contours of industrial dereliction.

12

Tipton

Tipton is worthy of a chapter to itself for not only is it a
traditionally large area of the central Black Country but here in
1966 two local men announced in the Press that they intended to
form a Black Country Society. They envisaged moderate interest
and were amazed at the response to a toe-in-the-water exercise
from which has stemmed a durable society which from the start
was a pressure group for founding a Black Country Museum – a
fact not always acknowledged now that the museum is a major
attraction.

Tipton is not an endearing name, the 'Tibbintone' of
Domesday sounding better to the ear, although the intervening
years have seen many variations in spelling until the present
form seems to have been adapted around the sixteenth century.
The old borough arms bear a crest of spearheads issuing from a
rock of stone, symbolizing heraldically the "tipps-stone",
presumably the nearest appropriate symbol available.

The Tipton recognized by local people includes Princes End,
Dudley Port, Great Bridge, Gospel Oak, Toll End, Ocker Hill and
other districts, and it is interesting to note that it once had seven
passenger railway stations and six good depots, indicating the
intense railway competition among nineteenth-century railway
companies. How many great cities could boast so many? Before
the railways there were canals so numerous that Tipton was
called 'the Venice of the Midlands', and despite some in-filling
over the years the waterways are still extensive.

Historically Tipton can claim an ecclesiastical 'first' since it has the oldest parish registers in England, dating to December 1513. The church of St Martin's is said to be medieval in origin. It stood in Upper Church Lane but in the middle of the eighteenth century the focal point of the village moved, and in 1797 a new church of the same name was built in Lower Church Lane, the latter being the parish church today, restored in 1963 and known locally as 'the Pepper Pot' by reason of its domed tower. However, the derelict body of the old church was rebuilt, the tower restored and upon completion in 1850 it was dedicated to St John: this church, the original St Martin's, is also still in use. Tipton's other churches are nineteenth-century apart from the Roman Catholic church in Victoria Road which is as recent as 1940.

Until the beginning of the eighteenth century the area consisted of meadow, pasture, woods and heath, and little had happened to disturb it until the Civil War, when in 1644 Parliamentary forces under Lord Denbigh advanced towards Dudley Castle from Wednesbury. King Charles at Worcester ordered one of his principal generals to take two thousand men to Dudley, and this superior force caused Denbigh to withdraw towards Tipton with the intention of 'putting themselves in order' prior to giving battle. The royalists attacked before their enemy was prepared, and a battle raged in which both sides suffered considerable losses. Whilst the result was indecisive, the castle was saved for the time being (in fact until May 1646), and the encounter passed into local lore as the Battle of Tipton Green.

Things would never be quite the same again, for already limestone was being quarried and the great South Staffordshire coalfield was beginning to stir: it has been calculated that by the year 1700 the Black Country was producing some seventy thousand tons of coal and a quantity of iron ore. But when it came to sinking pits, Tipton was and always would be in trouble from water, which is why the first-ever Newcomen engine was installed there in 1712 – we have seen the importance given to this event by the erection of a replica at the museum. As a pumping engine it was of limited value, and it was left to the later Boulton and Watt engines to enable mines over four hundred feet deep to be worked by the end of the eighteenth century. Evidence of the continued water problem can be gleaned from the fact that in 1854 local coalmasters were forced to get together and agree to share the cost of pumping out their mines. By 1920 either the best of the coal had been won or the battle with water was lost – probably an element of both – for by then coalmining in the district had virtually ceased, and it was claimed in 1938, when Tipton became a borough, that flooding, far from being disastrous, had turned out to be an advantage since it removed the danger of subsidence and made it safe to erect works and other buildings. Over-optimistic? A report issued in 1984 with regard to the same site on which the Newcomen engine is believed to have been installed said that twenty-five acres would have to be abandoned because of mineshafts and limestone workings, and it could not even be used as parkland because of the possible dangers. Thirty-seven uncapped mineshafts had been discovered, yet another legacy left by the extractive industries.

As to ironmaking, one of the most famed ironworks in Tipton was at Bloomfield, founded by Joseph Hall in 1830. It became known as Barrows & Hall, the largest producer of iron in the Black Country, the brand name BBH being one of the best known of all the iron trade marks. The works survived to 1906. But the industrial accolade as far as Tipton is concerned goes to the former Horseley Iron Company, where in 1821 the world's first iron steamship was built – the *Aaron Manby*, named after a partner in the firm. The dismantled vessel was sent to London by canal, reassembled and subjected to trials on the River Thames, whereupon the Press described it as being 'the most complete piece of workmanship in the iron way that has ever been witnessed'. The ship sailed to France and entered races with boats of a French company, but things didn't go according to plan: there were too many passengers, the coal was of unsuitable quality and so forth. Even so, this was an historic vessel, stated to have been broken up in France in 1855. Tipton is about as far as one can get from the sea in England, and the 150th anniversary of the sailing of the *Aaron Manby* was seized upon by the Black Country Society as being worthy of a special commemorative postal cover as well as of issuing a medallion. The Horseley works still exists as part of a large group of companies.

To strangers the best-known part of Tipton is Dudley Port, for many thousands will be aware of passing through on the main railway line even though they may not have heard of Tipton or indeed of the Black Country. The name 'Dudley Port' is a misnomer and goes back to the days of canal construction. As already explained, no canal could pass over Dudley's ridge at surface level without an unacceptable flight of locks, so the Birmingham-Wolverhampton canal at its nearest point become the on/off loading point for goods to and from the town – hence Dudley Port. Since the main railway line also missed Dudley, a branch line was built and the so-called 'Dudley Dodger' shuttled between Dudley Station and Dudley Port, making the four-minute journey some twenty-five times daily. Nowadays one has to catch a bus.

Whilst districts such as Great Bridge and Princes End have their own shopping areas, the centre of Tipton has always been regarded as Owen Street, a once bustling street of shops between the 'old line' canal at Factory Road and the gates of the level crossing. During the early 1980s Owen Street changed out of all recognition, the whole of the south side being demolished and replaced by a small modern shopping area and a rash of houses in the dark-red brick so beloved of today's architects. This is a conservation area on which much thought has been expended, and whilst the result is pleasing to many conservationists, it is certainly no longer the Owen Street that people remember. Development is incomplete but the most prized building is safe – the Fountain Inn on the corner of Factory Road. Restored in 1984, the inn is notable as having been for a time the headquarters of the Tipton Slasher.

Who was this Slasher who prefixed his nickname with the town of his birth? A murderer who attacked his victims with a knife? What nonsense! He was the legendary William Perry, champion prize fighter of England from 1850 to 1857. Born in 1819 Perry worked on narrow boats, as his parents had done, and quickly learned to fight other boatman in the mad scramble to be first through locks. Whilst in his early teens he was given undisputed priority of the waterways by virtue of his prowess with his fists, and in 1836 he fought and beat a Birmingham pugilist during which his reputation was established and he earned his nickname by using a slashing round right-arm blow. Within a decade he won several major fights and earned a tremendous reputation. When he became Champion of England, he retired and acquired a public house at West Bromwich. One day he consulted a fortune-teller known as 'the Dudley Devil' and was told:

Slasher, yo'll stop as yo' started.
Yo'll get all yo' gi'ed in one goo;
Yo' an' yer pub will be parted,
Tom Little will mek it cum true.

And so it proved, for in 1857 Tom 'Little', in the person of Tom Sayers, a man only five feet eight inches tall (hence little), challenged the Slasher for the championship, and out of condition as he was, and against the advice of friends, he not only accepted but gambled his pub, his furniture, rings and trophies. Sayers won after only ten rounds, and the reign of the last of the great bare-knuckle prize-fight champions was over. Perry died in 1880 and is buried in St John's churchyard, Kate's Hill, Dudley. A memorial tablet was erected as recently as 1925, indicative of the extent to which he is remembered. His grave is still visited by fight enthusiasts.

Much later another Tipton man made his mark in sporting history – long-distance runner Jack Holden. Born in 1907, he joined the Tipton Harriers and carried the name of the club and his town thoughout the world. In 1950 he won both Commonwealth and European marathons plus the AAA championships. He retired in the following year, and the Jack Holden Gardens opposite the public baths in Queen's Road was opened in his honour. The Tipton Harriers have produced many fine runners since the club was formed in 1910, an important step in its history being in 1971 when the Tipton Sports Centre was officially opened by the Duke of Edinburgh. Situated in Gospel Oak Road, its nineteen acres offer facilities for a whole range of sports.

Tipton folk have always played an enthusiastic part in whatever sport or entertainment was prevalent and like the rest of the region participated in bull-baiting and cock-fighting for years after they were officially banned. The once renowned Tipton Wakes are said to have exceeded all other festivals in revelry. If one is to believe local historians of the time, even the threat of the dreaded cholera did not deter them, which could be why the outbreak of 1832 was so severe that there were 404 deaths. Drunkenness was rife, and if it is thought that no Black Country person was sufficiently erudite as to spell bacchanalia – wrong! A poster of 1889 advertised 'a great bacchanalian demonstration held under the auspices of HRH King Alcohol, who has engaged the services of His Satanic Majesty The Devil to preside over the affair in order to render it effective'. How could it fail with that level of promotion despite the fervent prayers of groups of valiant Methodists? By the beginning of this century the wakes had mellowed to a more conventional funfair, surviving until 1959 when the fairground was built upon.

For more sedate pleasures Tipton has two parks, the Jubilee Park in the Toll End area and Victoria Park off Park Lane and close to Owen Street. This is the superior park opened in 1901 and true to form was a mining area with shafts to be filled in and a mound of spoil to be removed. The park boasts a large lake, which gave rise to a local joke that when the council were discussing the purchase of a gondola, the then mayor said, 'Why don't we have two and breed off them?'

Victoria Park is enhanced rather than marred by having a public library situated in one corner, the reason being that it is a very attractive building opened in 1906 and rightly said by Pevsner to be 'quite spectacular compared with what else Tipton has to offer'. There was an outcry in 1982 when it was learned that it was to close for economic reasons, and the Black Country Society along with other groups managed to get it reprieved.

Large as Tipton is, there is not a great deal to attract the visitor: housing estates include Tibbington, thereby perpetuating the ancient name, and another commonly known as 'the Lost City' because, once strangers get in, they have difficulty in getting out. Tipton shared with Dudley the distinction of producing Bean vehicles, and the original Bean works (now part of British Leyland) occupies Hurst Lane, part of the main Dudley-Wednesbury road. Even Great Bridge is a disappointment, being merely a stretch of the Dudley-West Bromwich Road with shops and a market. Alas, no great bridge, although no shortage of canal and river bridges. Great Bridge is in fact said to be a corruption of 'Greet', the name given to the River Tame in the Middle Ages, when there would have been a bridge of some kind.

However, Tipton does possess the one public house in the Black Country to bear the name of the region. In 1976, when a pub called the Britannia in Lower Church Lane was being renovated, it was thought that a change of name would be appropriate. What better than 'The Blackcountryman'?

13

Filling In

No matter how one carves up a congested area like the Black Country for the convenience of chapters, there are bound to be gaps. What follows is a brief run-down of localities not hitherto mentioned, although the knowledgeable will still be able to pinpoint small omissions. Complete blanket coverage is not the aim.

Wednesfield
Wednesfield, now part of Wolverhampton, was once proud of its independence as one of the oldest of the fringe Black Country communities, being little more than a hamlet until the coming of the canals in the eighteenth century. Its inhabitants worshipped at St Peter's in Wolverhampton, a two-mile walk, until St Thomas's was built as a chapel of ease in 1750. It was destroyed by fire in 1902 and promptly rebuilt around the surviving tower. Metalworking and engineering industries developed, and in particular large animal traps for hunters were made and exported worldwide. This unusual industry is reflected at the Black Country Museum, where a Wednesfield trap works has been rebuilt brick by brick.

After 1950 Wednesfield began a building programme which was to turn it into an overspill area for Wolverhampton, the population zooming from 17,400 in 1951 to some 28,000 in 1958. Although it resisted being turned into a dormitory suburb, it was invariably swallowed up. However, it has pleasant aspects, with

parks and playing fields, and being on the edge of the
conurbation has the splendid vastness of Cannock Chase within
easy reach. Wolverhampton's New Cross Hospital falls just
outside the old Wednesfield boundary. Built in the nineteenth
century as a workhouse for five hundred inmates, it became a
hospital in 1909 and developed into a major complex, the last
surviving parts of the original structure being demolished in
1979.

Rowley Regis

Rowley Regis village, as opposed to the old borough which was
centred on Old Hill, is a straggling hillside place on some of the
highest ground in the Black Country, situated on the 'top' road
south from Dudley to Birmingham via Blackheath. The name
probably derives from the Anglo-Saxon word '*ruh*' meaning
'rough', with the usual '*leah*' added, a combination easily
transposed to 'Rowley'. We are told that the twelfth-century
Pipe Rolls show Rowley as having been in the possession of the
king but the addition of the word '*regis*' cannot be traced beyond
the fourteenth century, and why such a bleak and isolated place
should be honoured with the appellation is difficult to imagine
since far more desirable parts of the region were in the monarch's
possession.

Little of historic interest remains, for although there has been
a church dedicated to St Giles from the thirteenth century, the
present building is the fourth to stand on the site. The original
survived until the early nineteenth century, and the controver-
sial Reverend George Barrs, who had married into the influential
Haden family of Haden Hill, is credited with getting it rebuilt in
1849. Disliked by many because of his alleged narrow-minded,
harsh and unsympathetic attitude, but certainly not lacking in
courage, he fought for his new church, describing the medieval
building as 'a cold, damp, ruinous and gloomy dilapidated
dungeon'. He died shortly after laying the foundation stone of
the new church, which in the event had a short life, being
considered unsafe in 1900 due to mining subsidence. The third
church, built in 1904, was destroyed by fire, the present structure
dating to 1923.

Early industry on the Rowley slopes consisted of farming,
nailmaking and mining, the underground wealth peculiar to the

region being unrecognized and unworkable commercially until the late nineteenth century – Rowley Rag, a very hard dolerite stone valuable for roadmaking and paving. It is still extracted in two deep excavations. A modern pub 'the Rowley Rag' proudly enshrines the mineral which geologists call basalt laccolith.

Blackheath

About a mile from Rowley in the direction of Birmingham the road drops down to Blackheath at the junction of major roads to Oldbury, the Cradleys, Halesowen, Dudley and Birmingham, a traffic bottleneck until new roads brought easement in 1984. Apart from local district signs, the name Blackheath is substituted by that of Rowley Regis so that it has virtually disappeared as a self-contained entity, although so far the streets of largely run-down shops are representatives of how the Black Country in general looked prior to post-war development.

Blackheath was originally a mining town and of little consequence before the middle of the last century, when it was simply a black heath, a meeting place of crude roads on the way to somewhere else. Incidentally, there is also a residential locality known as Whiteheath, situated on the slopes of the Rowley hills as they drop down to that Birmingham-Wolverhampton 'New' Road of 1927 vintage as it passes through Oldbury. These heights offer excellent panoramic views of the eastern Black Country and the broad sweeps of the motorway network.

Pensnett

Pensnett is a relatively small area between Kingswinford and Dudley, all that remains to remind one of the vast Pensnett Chase which existed prior to the middle of the eighteenth century and extended to present-day Kingswinford, Brierley Hill and Dudley Wood as well as outside the Black Country to the west. 'Pensnett' is said to derive from a combination of 'Penn', meaning a hill, and 'snett', signifying woodland, the earliest record of the name being in the thirteenth century. Its present focal point is High Oak on the Kingswinford-Dudley Road, but its industrial heart is a trading estate of around three hundred units encompassing that area of Shut End where the industrial railway referred to in Chapter 3 was ecstatically heralded by the

appearance of *The Agenoria* in 1829. A nice touch is the erection
of a pit-head frame and brick engine house at the south entrance
to the trading estate as a reminder of the district's mining past.

There was a mission church in Pensnett before the present
church of St Mark was built in 1846, and the first register of
Baptists dates from 14 December 1844. The surrounding mines
and ironworks quickly caused deterioration, and despite
restoration work throughout the 1870s it was merely a holding
operation, for by the turn of the century the structure was being
drawn out of shape. Eventually it seemed that demolition and
rebuilding were the only answer, but somehow the church was
completely restored during the 1920s, a mammoth task. Further
restoration was necessary in the 1950s. The most unusual feature
in St Mark's, a symbol of strife rather than peace, is a sword that
had once belonged to William Ewart Gladstone, the Victorian
Prime Minister who had had the misfortune to become involved
in the Oak Farm works. An inscription tells us that the sword
was actually made at these works. The church is reached along a
no-through road and lies behind a small park.

Himley

Himley is yet another village listed in Domesday as belonging to
William Fitz Ansculf, Lord of Dudley. It is still small, with a
population of under four hundred, bisected by the Kid-
derminster-Wolverhampton Road, having no shopping centre
and consisting of cottages, a recovery home, two public houses
and the extensive walled estate of Himley Hall. The present hall
was built in 1740 and was the family seat of the earls until 1838,
when Witley Court, near Stourport in Worcestershire, was
purchased. The decision to move further into the countryside
was prompted by the erection of Stephen Glynne's Oak Farm
works, which were too near for comfort; however, the hall
remained in the family and came into its own again after the Oak
Farm works had had their day. In 1919 the hall was modernized
and until 1939 was frequently visited by royalty. The Earl was a
friend of the Prince of Wales (later Edward VIII), and the Prince
often stayed at Himley. He also came as King in 1936, when he
planted a Cedar of Lebanon tree in the grounds, and Queen
Mary visited the hall in 1939. However, Himley Hall really hit
the national headlines in 1934 when the late Duke and Duchess

of Kent stayed there for the first part of their honeymoon.

The hall was purchased by the National Coal Board in 1947 and was used as a headquarters for twenty years, after which it was bought jointly by the Dudley and Wolverhampton authorities, who used it for education purposes. The grounds are open to the public, and a miniature village has been constructed. Only one small piece of ground belongs to the Earl of Dudley, and that is the Memory Garden in the grounds of the hall, a very private place to which the public rarely have access. It reflects the tragic side of the Dudley family in modern times, for this garden and the temple within were designed by Rosemary, Viscountess Ednam (daughter-in-law of the 2nd Earl), in memory of her seven-year-old son Jeremy who was killed in a car accident in London in 1929. In the following year she herself was killed in a plane crash, and she lies buried here alongside her son. Other graves in this quiet corner include those of the 2nd Earl, who died in 1932, and his wife, the famous actress Gertie Millar, who died in 1952.

Himley's church of St Michael and All Angels is a gem. Built of blue brick with concrete rendering, it was consecrated in 1764 and incorporated panelling and a rood screen from the earlier private chapel attached to the hall. There are many interesting tablets and memorials, and of particular interest is a standard depicting the coat of arms of the earls of Dudley. The lychgate was provided by the parishioners to commemorate Queen Victoria's Diamond Jubilee, and it is said that paupers and the unbaptized were buried beneath a large yew tree in the churchyard.

One can easily be overawed by the feeling of history which pervades both hall and church. This home of the earls in its rural setting on the edge of the Black Country is steeped in all that was good and bad in the development of the region. In retrospect the nineteenth-century earls in particular can be accused of everything that was inhuman in the treatment of their workers, but it certainly did not appear so then, and they were frequently applauded for their munificent gifts of land and money, mainly for churches. The present earl does not live in the region but shows a keen interest in local events and was one of the initial trustees of the Development Trust formed to construct and manage the Black Country Museum.

Postscript: Tourism

Despite the scars of industrial dereliction, with nearly a thousand acres of factory land lying idle in the mid 1980s, the four county boroughs responsible are dedicated to a face-lift designed to put more green into the Black Country and to encourage tourism.

To many people a less likely area of Britain to attract the tourist may seem hard to imagine, for there is little of scenic beauty, no backdrop one would wish to roll up and take away. But the attempt is genuine and has the backing of the Tourist Board. In 1985 Black Country Heritage Weekends were introduced, pin-pointing Stourbridge glassmaking and engraving, limestone fossil history and 'real ale' among the attractions. Organized bus tours cover such places as the Crooked House, Mushroom Green Chainshop and the Broadfield House Glass Museum.

The Black Country Museum and the zoo on Dudley's castle hill combine to form a focal point for visitors because of their close proximity, and ambitious plans are projected to develop further this part of Dudley as a major leisure complex. Thus, whilst the present-day Dudley Metropolitan Borough, which includes Stourbridge, Halesowen and much else besides, holds the chief potential, other areas are gearing up their attractions. For example Oak House, West Bromwich, the extensive Sandwell Valley, which includes the medieval 'sans well', Willenhall Lock Museum and Walsall's traditional leatherworks all have a contribution to make, not forgetting the widespread canal system which is being tidied, highlighting a legacy which in the main, surprising though it may seem, is actually older than the American Declaration of Independence and consequently of the USA.

In short, considerable effort is being made to make the region presentable in the midst of what is still a major industrial base, although the heavy industries have largely given way to the small factory unit and unemployment is high. A balance is being struck in which even Aynuk and Ayli have a place, but there must surely be an inherent danger in living off the past.

Bibliography

Barnsby, G.J., *Social Conditions in the Black Country 1800–1900* (Integrated Publishing Services, 1980)

Boulton, J., *Powered Vehicles Made in The Black Country 1900-1930s* (Black Country Society, 1976)

Burritt, E., *Walks in the Black Country and its Green Borderland* (1868; republished by the Roundwood Press, 1976)

Chandler and Hannah, *Dudley* (Batsford, 1949)

Chitham, E., *The Black Country* (Longman, 1972)

Church, R.A., *Kenricks in Hardware* (David & Charles, 1969)

Drabble, P., *The Black Country* (Robert Hale, 1952)

Ede, J.F., *A History of Wednesbury* (Wednesbury Corporation, 1962)

Fletcher, K., *The Old Testament in Black Country Dialect*, parts 1 and 2 (Black Country Society, 1975 and 1979 respectively)

Gale, W.K.V., *The Black Country Iron Industry* (Iron and Steel Institute, 1966)

Green, H.E., *The Limestone Mines of Walsall* (Black Country Society, 1977)

Millward and Robinson, *The West Midlands* (Macmillan, 1971)

Pevsner, N., *The Buildings of England – Staffordshire* (Penguin, 1974) *The Buildings of England – Worcestershire* (Penguin, 1968)

Raybould, T.J., *The Economic Emergence of the Black Country* (David & Charles, 1973)

Somers, F. and K.H., *Halas, Hales, Halesowen* (H. Parkes, 1932)
    Victoria Country Histories of Staffordshire and Worcestershire, various volumes (Oxford University Press)
Timmins, S., *The Resources, Products and Industrial History of Birmingham & The Midland Hardware District, 1886* (Republished by Frank Cass, 1967)
Willmore, F., *A History of Walsall* (1887; republished by S.R. Publishers, 1972)
Wright/Priddey, *Heart of England* (Robert Hale, 1973)

The Blackcountryman – quarterly magazine of the Black Country Society, established 1968.

Index